"René Daumal's *Rasa* is a transmission which reveals the first teachings on theatrical art, the Bhratya Natya Sastra. *Rasa* presents Daumal's views on poetry, Eastern philosophy, and Vedic texts in an inspiring and devotional manifesto. Louise Landes Levi is an ideal translator for this work, able to convey its meticulous analysis of the aesthetic and spiritual traditions of ancient India, through Daumal's brilliant and unique point of view."

—Tony Torn, actor-director
Ubu Sings Ubu

"For all practitioners of the sacred arts of India, René Daumal's *Rasa* is required reading. Illuminated with insight and inspiration, the translator Louise Landes Levi's *Rasa* is a portal; it is a pathway to understanding the aesthetic theory underlying all Indian arts. As a musician, singer, poet, and writer, Levi has the unique affinity and experience to bring this work to light."

—Barbara Framm, dance-master & exponent Bharata Natya & Odissi

"It's good to see this pioneering paradigmatic classic on Sanskrit and Indian culture in print again. Louise Landes Levi deserves a medal!"

—Peter Lamborn Wilson, writer, poet and editor
Temporary Autonomous Zone,
Pirate Utopias, Critique of the Image

RENÉ DAUMAL: SELECTED WORKS IN ENGLISH

Le Contre-Ciel (Le contre-ciel)
Le Contre-Ciel: The Anti-Heaven, Part One
Le Contre-Ciel: The Anti-Heaven, Parts Two and Three
A Fundamental Experiment
The Lie of the Truth and Other Parables from the Way of Liberation
Mount Analogue
Mugle and the Silk (Mugle; La soie)
A Night of Serious Drinking (La grande beuverie)
Pataphysical Essays
The Powers of the Word (1927–1943) (Les pouvoirs de la parole)
Rasa or Knowledge of the Self: Essays on Indian Aesthetics and Selected Sanskrit Studies
You've Always Been Wrong (Tu t'es toujours trompé)
René Daumal: Letters on the Search for Awakening, 1930-1944

RASA

RASA
or Knowledge of the Self

Essays on Indian Aesthetics
and Selected Sanskrit Studies

RENÉ DAUMAL

Edited
by
Claudio Rugafiori

Translated
by
Louise Landes Levi

Third Edition

Cool Grove Press

© 2023 Louise Landes Levi

Cool Grove Press, an imprint of Cool Grove Publishing, Inc. New York.
512 Argyle Road, Brooklyn, NY 11218

All rights reserved under the International and
Pan-American Copyright Conventions.
No part of this publication may be reproduced, stored in or
introduced into a retrieval system, transmitted or photocopied for distribution
without the prior permission of the Publisher.
All inquiries should be sent to info@coolgrove.com

www.coolgrove.com

THIRD EDITION
[FIRST COOL GROVE PRESS EDITION]
ISBN: 978-1-887276-41-2
Library of Congress Control Number: 2021937449

Front cover art is from *Five Senses* by **Francesco Clemente**, 1990.
Gouache on twelve sheets of handmade Pondicherry paper joined with
handwoven cotton strips, 237.5 x 242.6 cm (93 1/2 x 95 1/2 in.).
Stedelijk Museum, Amsterdam, Netherlands.
Special thanks to Raymond Foye
for his assistance with the work.

Selections in this book are from the following works by René
Daumal, originally published in French by Éditions Gallimard,
Paris:

    Les Pouvoirs de la parole, 1972
    L'Evidence absurde, 1972
    Bharata, 1970
    Le Contre-Ciel, 1970

& unpublished manuscripts from the archives of René Daumal.

The first edition of *Rasa* was translated from Sanskrit by René
Daumal, edited by Claudio Rugafiori, later translated into English
by Louise Landes Levi, and was published by New Directions,
NY, © 1982-2002, Louise Landes Levi, both as a hardcover and
a paperback.

A second edition was privately printed as a softcover book by
Shivastan in Kathmandu, Nepal, in a limited edition of 324 copies
in 2003 & then reprinted in 2006.

"On Indian Music" and "Concerning Uday Shankar" appeared in
the Uday Shankar Memorial Issue of The Journal of the Sangeet
Natak Akademi, Delhi, 1978.

Special thanks to
Rene Joseph Cote III for recreating the entire copy from a previously printed edition,
and to David Schonberger for proofing and editorial assistance.

Media Alchemy by Kiku

Cool Grove Press, NY

*This edition of RASA
is dedicated to the great
music master of the 1900s
Baba Allauddin Khan,
to his son Ustad Ali Akbar Khan,
&
to his daughter Shrimata Annapurna Devi*

ACKNOWLEDGEMENTS

*For this new edition,
the translator would like
to especially thank
Paul Leake,
for his
generous contribution,
to the reprint of
RASA,*

*Francesco Clemente
& Raymond Foye,
for the cover art,*

*Tej Hazarika
the publisher of Cool Grove
&
all the musicians, dancers, poets & friends
who in times of distress work
to maintain the RASAs
as embodiments
of the essence of artistic
empowerment & expression.*

*LLL
Kyoto 2021*

The path of knowledge is only to drive inwards with the mind, not uttering the word "I," and to question whence, as "I," it rises. To meditate "This is not I" or "That I am" may be in aid, but how can it form the enquiry?

When the mind, inwardly enquiring "Who am I?" attains the heart, something of itself manifests as "I-I," so that the individual "I" must bow in shame. Though manifesting, it is not "I" by nature, but perfection, and this is the self.

Sri Ramana Maharshi

Acknowledgments

The translator would like to thank the many friends and associates who assisted in the translations of this selection from the writings and studies of René Daumal, in particular, Claudio Rugafiori, secretary of the Daumal Archives, H. J. Maxwell, Henri Michaux, Yvette Moch, Denise de Casabianca-Goldenberg, and P. Makriaamos, who proofread the original text; Richard Leigh, Noel Cobb, and the English playwright Heathcote Williams, who thoroughly edited the English text. Simon and Barbara Vinkenoog, Frans and v. c. Leeuwe, Robert Beer, and many others who directly contributed to the conditions which permitted the completion of this text. And the various schools and their methods of self-study, in India and Europe, which provided the living sonority to which Daumal was dedicated.

RASA
or Knowledge of the Self

TABLE OF CONTENTS

Foreword, by Louise Landes Levi xv
Introduction, by Louise Landes Levi xvii

TO APPROACH THE HINDU POETIC ART . . 1
ON INDIAN MUSIC 17
CONCERNING UDAY SHANKAR 29

THE ORIGIN OF THE THEATER
OF BHARATA 39
   A Translation of the Natya Sastra 44
   Notes on the Translation of the Natya Sastra 56

ORIENTAL BOOK REVIEWS
   The Tibetan Book of the Dead 67
   The Life of Marpa, "The Translator" 73
   Buddhism, Its Doctrines and Methods 76
   Two Tibetan Texts on the Conversion of the Birds . . . 78
   Hymns and Prayer of the Veda 82

THE HYMN OF MAN
   A "Vertical" Translation 85
   Notes: Extracts from the Commentaries of
   Sridhara and Sayana 96

TO THE LIQUID
   Extract from the Rig Veda 99
   Hymn LXIX 101
   Rig Veda ("The Vision of the Stanzas") 104

KNOWLEDGE OF THE SELF
   Extract from the Brihadaranyaka Upanishad 107

SOME SANSKRIT TEXTS ON POETRY
   1. *The Utility of Poetry* 109
   2. *The Essence of Poetry* 113
   3. *The Savor* 116
   Appendix

THE FOUR CARDINAL TIMES 121
About the Translator 122

AFTERWORD
   A Form of Fire 124

FOREWORD

René Daumal (b. 1908) is best known for his novel *Mount Analogue*, unfinished at his death in 1944 (other works in English include *A Night of Serious Drinking* and *The Powers of the Word*). Daumal was an autodidact, i.e., a non-academic, Sanskritist. Following youthful explorations with poet Gilbert-Lecomte (*Black Mirror*) and initial instruction in Sanskrit from René Guénon he embarked on a solitary study, surpassed his teacher, and eventually formulated his own Sanskrit dictionary. He translated essential texts on Sanskrit composition, poetry in Sanskrit, including the famous hymn concerning *Soma*, and the first chapter of the *Bharatya Natya Sastra*, the world's first treatise on the dramatic arts, written circa 4th century. Writing numerous essays on Sanskrit poetics, his deeply felt intention was to present these texts and the spiritual etymology of the sub-continent in a form accessible to the 'common man,' and to the artists and new societies of the 20th century.

As secretary to Uday Shankar, he wrote the first reviews of Indian music and dance in the West (Paris, circa 1935) and accompanied Uday Shankar's troupe, which included Ravi Shankar as a 12-year-old dancer, to NYC. During the 2nd World War, exiled in the South of France with his wife Vera, who was Jewish, he furthered his literary work, completing essays, translations, and reviews, while maintaining, with others so exiled, a profound epistolary exchange (see Letters

1930-1944), until his death from tuberculosis, shortly before the Allied landing.

RASA, a 'cult classic' edited by Claudio Rugafori, secretary of the Daumal archives and translated by American poet and musician, Louise Landes Levi, has earned its reputation. The forthcoming edition with Cool Grove Press (2022) is its third, prior editions being New Directions, 1982 and Shivastan, 2003 and 2006.

<blockquote>—reprinted from Blank Forms Journal, Issue no. 7, Introduction to Daumal's Poetry Black/Poetry White</blockquote>

INTRODUCTION

René Daumal was born in Charleville in the Ardennes in 1908 and died of tuberculosis in 1944 in Paris, France. His adult life was dedicated to an inner work of the highest rigor and to the completion of his essays, poems, novels, and translations. He founded, with Roger Gilbert-Lecomte and several others, a journal of experimental metaphysics and poetry entitled *Le Grand Jeu*, recently reprinted in France by Jean-Michel Place and edited by C. Rugafiori and H. J. Maxwell. He mastered Sanskrit and translated a selection of important texts from the *Sahitya-darpana*, the *Chandogya Upanishad*, the *Bhagavad Gita*, etc. Most of these translations have been reprinted in *Bharata*, edited by J. Masui and published by Éditions Gallimard in 1970. Daumal also wrote a Sanskrit grammar, *Traité de grammaire et de poétique sanskrite*, published, in a facsimile edition, in Paris in 1980.

Daumal did not intend with his study of Sanskrit an institutional process which would result in economic gain or academic position. Rather he pursued the subject as a personal search and research, a "proof," a necessary corollary to his youthful experimentation with carbon tetrachloride and other stimulants (described in his essay "Le Souvenir determinant," 1943, and in an earlier edition of this article "Une Experience fondamentale"). His interest in intoxicants, their relation to the inner state and to the origin of language was curtailed, however, by his meeting with Alexandre de Salzmann and his subsequent contact with the Gurdjieff Institute in Paris.

"And above all, remember the day when you wanted to throw out everything, no matter how—but a guardian kept watch in your night, he kept watch while you dreamed, he made you touch your flesh, he made you gather your rags—remember your guardian."[1] Daumal continued his studies with the Institute from 1929 until his death, and his writing, particularly his essays on poetics, was deeply colored by his work with this school.

In 1929 and 1930 Daumal worked as Uday Shankar's secretary on Shankar's first performing tour of the West. Shankar was accompanied by his troupe of Indian dancers and musicians, and their performances were Western Europe's first exposure to Indian dance and music. The essays "On Hindu Music" and "Concerning Uday Shankar" are thus historic pieces, written pre-eminently to clarify these performances to a naïve Occidental audience, and to an inimical critical appraisal. Daumal traveled to America with the Shankar company and upon his return married Vera Milanova, a highly educated woman of Russian descent who was deeply in sympathy with his intellectual and spiritual work.

Daumal remained in France from 1932 to 1944, living in a great variety of circumstances due to his failing health and the approach and advent of World War II. Vera was partly Jewish, and thus the Occupation was spent in hiding until his death in May 1944, two weeks before the Allied landing. Despite the strain and uncertainty of this period, however, Daumal explored an entire range of literary expression and furthered his knowledge of Oriental philosophy and language. The Sanskrit study was, until his death, a major aspect of Daumal's desire to reconstitute, within himself, the Occidental approach to poetic expression and to resuscitate, in an Occidental framework, the essence of sacred art and perception. Daumal sought a poetry which would awaken the poet to his internal reality, not only to the word, tool, and result of that reality. In his essay *Poetry Black, Poetry White*, written in 1942, he said, "I will not say 'he' is a white poet and 'he' is a black. This would be to fall from the idea into opinion, discussion and error. I will not even say 'he' has the poetic gift … and 'he' not. Do I have it? Often I doubt it and sometimes I believe it absolutely. I am never certain once and for all. Each moment the question is new. Each time the dawn appears the mystery is there in its entirety. But if formerly I was a poet, certainly I was a black poet and if tomorrow I were to be a poet I would like to be a white poet."[2] He formulated a theory of poetic expression in which his researches into the Oriental tradition were brought to bear upon the poetic tradition of the Oriental world. Here an Occidental yoga of poetry is evolved, based not only on the form and content of expression but on a conscious inner process corresponding to an awakened approach to creativity. "White poetry opens the door to one world, that of the only sun, without illusion, real."[3]

Daumal's translation of Sanskrit texts which deal with poetry and composition directly inspired his future work in these areas. In Sanskrit the word is not only a tool of poetic expression, but it is in its esoteric usage the poet's mirror and the mirror of the gods. The Sanskrit alphabet is a sacred formula whose function is, in addition to the complexity of its compositional forms, the direct reflection of the sacred world and its powers. "All recited poems and all chants are, without exception, portions of Vishnu, the great being, reclothed in sonorous form."[4] From the time of Panini (4th century B.C.) Sanskrit was regarded as a perfected vehicle–*samskrta*.

It was not subject to development but was considered, by its exponents, to be a direct form of being, in itself an expression of sacred power. Thus, in India, other languages are known as *Prakrtas*, natural tongues, which are subject to evolution, but Sanskrit was a fixed expressive form whose potency, exoterically and esoterically, was utilized to develop, record, and reveal man's inner nature. The science of *mantra,* indeed the entire science governing Sanskrit exposition, derives from its unique capacity to create and reflect the state of conscious being. As Daumal states, many of its most revered compositions date from an unrecorded period and are held to be anonymous, or rather, to be the result of a direct process of reception, unrelated to personal authorship.

Daumal's translation work reflects his desire to place this ancient tradition at the service of the European literary intelligence. His translation of Bharata's *Natya Sastra,* considered to be the first written treatise on the arts of poetry, music, and dance, into a vital, living French attests to this deeply felt motive—one which would give to Occidental culture an image of its origin and of an artistic form and formula which existed not to distract but to "awaken"—to awaken man to consciousness of himself. His book reviews, concerned primarily with sacred works translated into French, were written for various literary reviews, *La Nouvelle Revue Française, Hermes II,* and *Fontaine.* His essay on the *Tibetan Book of the Dead,* written for *Les Cahiers du Sud* in 1934, is considered, among his short works, to be a masterpiece.

If the style of the following translations, essays, book reviews, and commentaries appears to be somewhat dry, or philosophic, it must be remembered that they represent only one aspect of Daumal's creative expression, which was otherwise devoted to fiction, occasional papers, translations (from English to Hemingway and D.T. Suzuki) and poetry. In all these expressions, however, Daumal's concern was uniquely dedicated to "the power of the word." His life task was consecrated to the silence of the inner world and to the discipline of that void—"one does not know the word by the medium of words but silence"[5]—and to the relevance of the word to the consciousness of man and to the individual, in particular, to the poet whose function is especially related to the phenomena of language, its origin and its creative potential.

The great majority of Daumal's work was not published, except in various reviews, in his lifetime, due to the exigency of the war years in France and to other factors, such as his health and his insistence that literary publication should meet and balance his financial needs. The Sanskrit essays and studies in this selection are drawn from a large collection of books, essays, reviews, notes, and translations, and by no means is this selection complete. However, from it one can surmise both the integrity and intellectual brilliance of Daumal.

His Sanskrit work, as stated, was autodidactic, a product of his unique sensibility and not the product of an academic tradition. Daumal sought within this study proof for the ultimate reality and expression which would indicate, not annihilate, the possibility for man to free himself from the pain of *samsara*—his own ego.

But Daumal's contribution, as shown, was by no means limited to Sanskrit translation, and his other works, two of which have been translated into English, *Mont Analogue* (*Mount Analogue*, City Lights, 1971) and *La Grande Beuverie* (*A Night of Serious Drinking*, Routledge & Kegan Paul, 1979 and Shambhala, 1979), attest to his humor and his unique approach to the situation of Western man. Nevertheless his Sanskrit study provided both an analytic tool and structural form for most of his other work, including his poetry, and *La Grand Beuverie* refers directly to this study. Beneath its surrealist guise the book is, in fact, an anagram, and the text cannot be followed without at least some knowledge of Daumal's research into the classical traditions and languages of the Orient.

As Daumal accompanied the first Indian performers on their tour of America, it is appropriate that his essays on poetry, music, and dance, in particular, be the first nonacademic interpretation of this material published in America. The translator is deeply grateful to Mr. James Laughlin of New Directions for his encouragement and support and to Jon and Lynne Weinberger whose photograph (see p. xvi) on the cover of this book genuinely completes its intention and is also witness to a rare friendship. And for Daumal, intellect and spirit did not obscure the heart, the reality of daily life upon which and from which liberation was conceived.

—Louise Landes Levi
London, June–November 1979

NOTES

[1] "*Memorables*" by René Daumal, translated by L.L. Levi, Maitreya, Vol. 4. 1974, Berkeley, CA.

[2] "*Poésie noire et poésie blanche,*" *Les Pouvoirs de la parole, Essais et Notes, II,* Paris: Éditions Gallimard, 1972 (no English translation available at present).

[3] Ibid.

[4] "*To Approach the Hindu Poetic Art*" by René Daumal, included in the present volume.

[5] "*Between Two Chairs*" by René Daumal, translated by L. L. Levi, *Text,* No. 7, 1978, New York, N.Y.

A NOTE ON SANSKRIT

Every letter of the Sanskrit alphabet is also a *bija* mantra—a seed syllable—whose energy is that of a particular *deva* or *devi* (god or goddess). These syllables manifest pure energy—sound in its direct derivation. For the practitioner they dissolve into light—his true nature, thus allowing him to transcend the mundane world as perceived by his ego-mind and to experience his absolute nondual nature, the self or *atma* in Sanskrit terminology.

TO APPROACH THE HINDU POETIC ART[*]

One day I saw that all those books had offered me only fragmentary plans of the palace. The first knowledge I acquired, painful and very real, was that of my prison. The first reality I experienced was that of my ignorance, my vanity, my laziness, of everything which bound me to the prison. And when I looked again at the images of the treasures which India, through books and intellect, had sent me, I saw why these messages remain incomprehensible.

We approach those ancient and living truths with our modern European psychic attitudes: there are thus perpetual opacities.

Modern man believes himself adult, complete, having no more to do, until death, than to gain and spend goods (money, vital forces, learning), without these transactions affecting that which calls itself "I." The Hindu[1] regards himself as an entity to complete, a false vision to rectify, a composite of substances to transform, a multiplicity to unify.

We regard knowledge as the specific activity of the intellect. For the Hindu, each of man's activities is seen as a participant in knowledge.

For us, the development of knowledge entails the acquisition, by perceptual and logical apparatus, of new information pertaining to things we can perceive or about which we can hear. In Hindu thought, the development of knowledge entails the perfecting of the apparatus and the organic acquisition of new faculties of understanding.

We say that to know is "to be able" and "to foresee." For the Hindu, it is to become and to transform oneself.

Our experimental method aspires to apply itself to all objects, *except* to the "self," which is rejected in the domains of philosoph-

---
[*]First published in *La Nouvelle Revue Française*, 1931. Later reprinted in *Bharata*, Paris, Éditions Gallimard, 1970.

ical speculation and religious faith. For the Hindu, the "self" is the first, last, and fundamental object of knowledge—not only experimental but transformative.[2]

We regard men as equal in *being* and different only in having innate qualities and acquired learning. The Hindu recognizes a hierarchy in the being of men: the master is not only more knowledgeable or more skillful than the student, he *is* essentially more. And it is this that makes possible the uninterrupted transmission of truth.

Finally, for modern man, the acquisition of knowledge is an activity that is separate, independent (or, desired to be so) from all others. For the Hindu, it is the transformation of man himself and implies a complete change in his personal expression, in his entire manner of living.

This change manifests itself according to the different human types (the original institution of caste),[3] according to the ages and stages of life (the rule of *karma*),[4] and according to the professions and social functions (the doctrine of *dharma*).[5] I do not have direct, practical access to the Vedic hymns, not being a Brahman, nor to the *Upanishads*, not being a *sannyasi*. I can only let myself be intermittently illumined by their rays. The texts of liturgy, architecture, strategy, law, veterinary art and the one hundred others whereby the one doctrine descends into the diverse human activities are not for me. But I am, by profession, a writer, and one day I would like to be a poet. The door that opens for me on the Hindu tradition is thus the science of language, rhetoric, and poetry.[6] By adhering to my *dharma* as a writer, I will be able to give practical content to the teachings of the books. In the following chapters, I will try to present an outline of the most fertile ideas that a writer can encounter in the Hindu texts of aesthetics and poetry.

The Origin of Art

Art is not a natural activity[7] of man. In the ages when knowledge of the real was the most important goal of human life, all natural activities were, at the same time, analogies, signs, proofs of the interior research. With the coming of the *kali-yuga*, the epoch of obscurity (in the middle of which we live), men began to practice these activities for their exterior fruits alone. Leading the cortege of passions, the pair "agreeable-disagreeable" became the principal motive of conduct. And, in the meantime, the inferior castes proliferated. The gods, it is said,[8] distressed by the ensuing disorder, prayed to Brahman to "produce a new Veda," a fifth, destined for all of the castes. "And, from the substance of the four *Vedas*, He-who-sees things-as-they-are created the Dramatic Art." The theater was to be an "analogy of the movement of the world,"[9] a condensed expression of "the three worlds," the universal laws, and the "four motives in human conduct": *artha*, "material prosperity, goods," motives of the physical plane; *kama*, "desire, passion," emotional motives; *dharma*, "duty," intellectual and moral motives; and *moksha*, "deliverance," the desire for liberation from the "three motives" and thus of a "supramundane" nature. All human types, all castes, all professions were to envision themselves within this system. Thus, each man could experience the profound pleasure of seeing himself represented, comprehended, placed in the total movement of the universe. Each person, fool or wise man, coward or hero, serf or lord, would see the justification for his existence in the harmony of the worlds, and, through the door of individual emotion, enter the sacred teaching.[10]

Thus, art was cast into the world by superior beings, intending to clothe the truth and to attract to it, by artifice, our spirits which had become incapable of loving it in the nude. The author of the *Mirror of Composition*[11] considers the same idea: "The knowledge of the four kinds of motives, as it is presented in the Vedic treatises, is already difficult for those whose reason is in full maturity, because it is presented without any savor... By virtue of poetry, it becomes accessible to those whose reason is still in a tender infancy..."

Art, therefore, is not an end in itself. It is a medium in service of sacred understanding. But if the Hindu art is made to represent the universal laws, to determine that "we conduct ourselves like Rama and his like and not like Ravana and his like,"[12] it is far from being didactic and moralizing. The instructive texts and books of morality address themselves to the intellect. Art, through emotion, seeks to animate the entire being. And it is not enough to say that art "represents" the universe; in fact, art remakes it, it recreates from it an analogy.

Two directly related principles are at the foundation of the aesthetic. The one—analagous recreation of the universe—is particularly apparent in the plastic arts. The other—the establishment of an emotional concord between the individual and the universal laws—manifests itself in music, dance, and poetry. The first is expressed through the concept of *pramana* (right proportion, analogic precision, conformity to the idea model)[13] in architecture, sculpture, and painting. The second is expressed in poetry through the concept of *rasa*, "savor," direct apprehension of a state of being.

The Doctrine of Language
Before attempting to follow the Hindu aestheticians into the ultimate poetic mysteries, where the verbal process is a reflection on himself of the poet's work, it is necessary to recall the artisan foundation of Hindu art. For the Hindu, the expression of the personality has no artistic value at all. The beautiful *is* the evocative power of truth.[14] The artist is, above all, an artisan, whose task is *to make* certain objects according to certain laws and with a certain goal. First, of course, he must know the material with which he works. Therefore, the poetic art is founded on a science and doctrine of language usage.[15]

Is there, between words and things, a rapport of simple convention or an eternal appropriateness? In India, as in Greece, both of these theses were supported. But the second, expounded by Bhartrihari,[16] does not exclude the first. According to Bhartrihari, two kinds of language exist. One is made from word-seeds (*sphota*), ideas, inalterables, that are modulations of the universal *atman*, the real divisions of the universe. The word *sphota* is the object in the relation of manifesting cause to manifested effect.[17] The other kind is created from sonorous words (*dhvani*), usual words, subordinated to natural laws, that is, to the rules of phonetics and grammar.[18] When Mammata and Visvanatha explain how conventional senses relate to words (by concomitance of perceptions, reflections, or direct teachings), and speak only of this natural and sensible language, this does not mean that they deny the reality of forms pre-existent to words and objects.

René Daumal

The doctrine of *sphota* is not easy to understand; and still, no doubt, withholds many of its mysteries from me. The existence of thought without words but not without forms is nevertheless necessary, for example, to all translation work. Every good translator does his utmost, without actually realizing it, to translate his text first into *sphota,* in order to retranslate into the second language; but he would be an even better translator if he were consciously aware of this process.

The Powers of the Word [19]
The material upon which the poet works is made up of vocables (*sabda*) and meanings (*artha*). A word (*pada*) is a vocable associated with a meaning. The "meaning" of the word is not a simple abstract designation: *artha* means "thing, object, value" but also "goal" as the psychological content of the word, the intention of the speaker, is a modulation of his "I." "The meaning" is also called "fruit" (*phala*) of the word when its effect on the auditor is considered.

"Words" have three kinds of meanings. That is to say, the "vocables" (which are words of power) have three "powers": they carry literal meanings, derived meanings (figurative, metaphoric), or suggestive meaning. In the literal meaning, a word designates a "genus," a "specific attribute," a "substance" (or individual being), or an "action" (or transitory quality). The derived meaning is engendered by an incompatibility between the literal meaning and its content ("the cow speaks"; "cow" being a nickname for the people from a particular country). This mechanism which resolves contradictory meanings into derived meanings is described with all the rigorous detail of the Hindu dialecticians.

These two kinds of meaning suffice for the needs of ordinary speech and didactic literature.[20] But if one analyzes a poem (recognized as such by "those who have a heart") and discerns the literal and derived meanings, a "surplus meaning" remains, differing from the preceding ones, not deducible by logical inference, and perceived, moreover, as the true meaning of the poem by "he who savors it." This meaning, this new "power" of the word, is called "resonance" (*dhvani*) or "suggestion" (*vyanjana*) or still "gustation"

5

(*rasana*). It is born from certain combinations of words whose interpretation by literal and derived meanings is insufficient. Here again, the psycholinguistic mechanisms by which "suggested meanings" give rise to yet other meanings is described and classified with a subtlety and analytic precision that is almost vertiginous.[21]

The Savor
But what is the content of this "suggestion," what resonates in this "resonance" and is, itself, the meaning of the poem? In other words, what, in essence, *is* poetry? Having refuted a certain number of definitions proposed by other authors,[22] Visvanatha says, "Poetry is a word whose essence is *savor*."[23] And he explains the meaning of "savor" (*rasa*): "A fundamental emotion such as love, manifested by the representation of its occasional causes, tangible accompaniments and effects, becomes 'savor' for those who have knowledge." Savor is not the base emotion, related to personal life; it is a "supernatural" (*lokottara*) representation, a moment of consciousness provoked by the mediums of art and colored with a particular pathos. Dare I say: an objective emotion? To our Occidental mentality, this would seem to be a strange notion, but if we recall the moments of intense aesthetic emotion that we have experienced, a certain "savor" will come to mind: and we will see how and why this gustative image asserts itself. The savor is essentially a cognition, "shining with its own evidence," thus immediate. It is "conscious joy" (*anandacinmaya*) … even in the representation of painful things; it is not related to the ordinary "world"; it is a recreation of that "world" on another plane. It is animated by "supernatural admiration." It is "the twin sister of the sacred gustation." "He who is capable of perceiving it, savors it not like a separate thing, but in its essence." It is "simple, like the taste of a complex dish."[24] It can only be grasped by men capable of judgment,[25] having a "power of representation"; it compels an act of "communion."[26] It is not an object existing before being perceived "like a pitcher that has been illumined with a lamp"; it exists to the degree that it has been savored. It is not the mechanical "effect" of the artistic means

which merely manifest it. It is not subject to our time (the *tri-kala—past-present-future*). It is not "of this world." One knows it only by savoring it.

The manifestation of "savor" is the linguistic function of the "power of suggestion."[27]

The concept of *rasa* is at the core of the Hindu aesthetic. I will make no commentary on the preceding citations. The illusion of having understood them would prevent me from seeking to understand them further, and this effort more fully to understand has always been the most fertile one for me.

The Analogy Poem-Man
The savor is the essence, the "self" (*atman*) of the poem. In the poem, as in man, the *atman* is manifested by certain "qualities" (*guna*) which are also called "functions, specific activities" (*dharma*) of the savor.[28] They are classified in three principal categories: *suavity*, that "liquifies the spirit," softens it; *ardor*, that "ignites the spirit," exalts it; *evidence*, that illumines the spirit "with the rapidity of fire in dry wood." The different kinds of poetic emotions are derived from these three categories.

Just as man's inner state expresses itself through certain attitudes, poetry expresses itself through "allures" (*riti*) which are directly related to the "qualities." Specific sonorities and stylistic forms correspond to each one. The sweet, easy "allure" develops the meaning of the phrase gradually from the first to the last word. The opposite, exultant "allure" keeps the audience in suspense until the last parts of the phrase which explosively illumine it.[29] And there are intermediary "allures," each one corresponding to an attitude which the poet wishes to convey to the auditor.[30] Thus, before composing a poem, the poet must compose himself, inwardly prepare to be the best possible receptacle for the savor. He must put aside that which we call the "personality," in order to master the impulses of his vanity and the caprices of his imagination.

The "body" of the poem is created from "sounds and meanings" which are subject to the laws of the three linguistic "powers." The material, upon which the poet works, is not only sonorous, it is psychological as well. The use of a word produces more than vocal sound; it releases a whole world of associations, of figurative and derived meanings and suggestions. It is thus necessary to know the linguistic laws. For he who knows them "a single word, well used and perfectly understood is, in Heaven and in the world, the sacred cow to fulfill all desire."

The poetic body, like the human one, has its "defects" (*dosha*), faults of "sound" and "meaning" which must insofar as possible be eliminated. It also has ornaments, rhetorical figures or "embellishments" (*alamkara*). The study of "embellishment" is given a major place in the poetic treatises.[31] Poetry, without embellishment, hardly exists, but when the embellishment is used for itself, the resulting poetry is considered to be in poor taste and of inferior quality.[32] The embellishment is legitimate as a sweet destined to "enhance the savor"; its real function, the profound intention of the poet who utilizes it, is the suggestion of savor. And thus, the image of a god with a flowered arc who pierces the hearts of the young is as evocative today or yesterday as it was a thousand years ago, for it has proved its value.

Prosody is also concerned with the "body" of the poem. But the Hindus never confuse metrics and poetry. Most of their didactic works are in verse, and although the poetry is usually metrical, it is not necessarily so. Metrics assume precise aesthetic value only in the chant. In poetry, that which corresponds to the concept of "rhythm" is not metrical form, limited to sounds, but "allures" which regulate the complex course of sounds and meanings, images and emotions; more generally, it is the way in which the poet conjoins these concurrent elements.[33]

In these notes, I hope to have shown that for the Hindu, poetry, if it is only a medium in the service of knowledge, is also one of the highest activities that can be practiced by man. "The state of man is difficult to attain in this world, and then knowledge is very difficult to attain. The state of the poet is difficult to attain and then, the creative power is very very difficult to attain."[34] The poetic process, of which the poetic gustation is a reflection, is the real work of the poet, not only the knowledge of his material and the rules of his profession but an inner work, to discipline and to order himself, so that he will be a better instrument for the "supernatural" functions—in sum, a kind of *yoga*. Through an interplay of sounds, meanings, resonances, allures, the poet's entire inner world is activated. And, as he is a reflected light of the universal *atman*, his poetic art participates in the cosmic motion. "All recited poems and all chants, are, without exception, portions of Vishnu, the Great Being, reclothed in sonorous form."[35]

I would like to have offered some examples, but their translation would not have been very meaningful. Each person can search for them, according to his own understanding, among the poets that he most admires, as the laws of the Hindu poetic are, in principle, valid for all languages. But, be careful. In Occidental poets, the power of suggestion, of *rasa*, manifests itself to a certain extent by chance; according to mechanisms that are poorly understood and which are classified according to the vague notion of "inspiration." The apprenticeship evolves without method and the results are accidental. The Hindu poet is the product of a methodical education, pursued beside a master, with a goal superior to art alone. The Occidental poet develops himself, for better or worse, without really understanding his process, and his talent nearly always crystallizes itself in the expression of emotions which most conform to his individual nature. Racine is a marvelous poet of the erotic, but almost, uniquely, in its various nuances. The Hindu poet, as an artisan, must be able to play the entire scale of each emotion. The difference is still more striking for the actor-dancer, but it is evident in all the arts.[36]

I would like to have shown how all Hindu arts are related; the theater contains them all. The corporeal analogy of the poem is not truly comprehensible without dance; painting, it is said, cannot manifest itself without dance, which cannot be understood without music;[37] in sculpture and in dance, one finds the same science of attitudes—the principles of which belong to *yoga*—and the same language through manual gestures ... I would like to have tried to say that according to what I have read and heard, the same principles of poetry govern dance, mimicry, and plastic arts. But nothing is so contrary to the Hindu genius as the treatment of subjects which one does not practically know. Ganesha would not have forgiven me.

—1943

René Daumal

NOTES

[1] "Hindu," here, as in the whole of this article, signifies: someone who recognizes the authority of the Vedic tradition. But the described mental attitudes would be those of anyone recognizing the authority of any other aspect of the universal tradition.

[2] From which the apparent multiplicity of the meanings of the word *atman* in classical Sanskrit. In Vedic, it is still related to the image of "vital breath." *Atman*, "self," is that with which the being identifies when it says "I." This can be the social and exterior personality or the body, feelings, and thoughts—all of this, illusion. For he who *makes himself*, the *atman* is the "master of the chariot," described in the *Katha Upanishad*, or the divine personage, or the absolute being. On this subject see the teachings of Prajapati in the *Chandogya Upanishad*.

[3] According to the *Rig Veda* (X, 91) when primordial man had been sacrificially dismembered, "his mouth was the *Brahman* (the sacerdotal caste), his arms became the royalty (the *Kshatriya* caste), his thighs were the *Vaisya* (the plebian class), and from his feet the *Sudra* (the servile caste) was born." An equivalent social and corporeal analogy is found in the *Republic* of Plato. See also the *Laws* of Manu, chapter 1.

[4] The teaching of the *Veda* is accessible first, to the *brahmacharin* ("studying the sacred science," from the investiture of the sacred cord made on the sixth day until marriage), in the form of rules of conduct, religious observances, and intellectual studies; second, to the *grihastha* ("Master of the house," from marriage to the state of grandfather), in the form of sacrificial art, mythology, and theology, in the *brahmanas*; third, to the *vanaprastha* ("inhabitant of the forest," an anchorite studying beside a master), in the form of interior sacrifice, in the *aranyaka*, "books of the forest"; fourth, finally, to the *sannyasin* ("renouncing," "surrendering the laws of the castes and stages of life"), in the most profound form of the "knowledge of the self," in the *Upanishads*. See Max Muller, *Origine et développement de la religion à la lumière des religions de l'Inde*, French translation by J. Darmesteter.

[5] Particularly revealed in the *Bhagavad Gita*. On the castes and the stages of life, see the *Laws* of Manu. The rejection of the castes and the *asrama* and the negation of the authority of the *Vedas* characterize the two great heresies, Jainism and Buddhism.

RASA or Knowledge of the Self

[6] A large door. For of all the ancient literatures, Sanskrit is the richest in this domain. Of the six annexed sciences, indispensable for the study of the *Vedas* (*vedanga*), four are related to language (phonetics, grammar, lexicology, metrics; the two others are ritual and astronomy). The monumental work of Panini (sixth or fifth century B.C.?) with its commentaries is full of teachings for modern phoneticians and grammarians. Paul Regnaud, in his *Rhétorique Sanskrite*, cites about forty works, often enriched with commentaries, related to rhetoric, dramatic composition, and poetry.

[7] *Prakrita*, "natural, produced from *prakriti*," as opposed to *samskrita*, "completed, deliberately made or remade," in a certain sense "consecrated." Thus, languages divide themselves into prakrit and sanskrit; man, as nature and the natural society make him, is *prakrita*, or still more *akritatman*, "who does not develop a self"; he becomes *samskrita* and *kritatman* through the sacred knowledge symbolized and actualized by the "sacraments" or *samskara*.

[8] In the First Reading of the *Natya Sastra*, "Treatise on the Theater," attributed to the *muni* Bharata. It is the most ancient authority on the subject of aesthetics (for the theater is total art), unanimously acknowledged by Hindu aestheticians up to the present time. I attempted a translation of this in *Origin of the Theater* for the review *Measures*, October 1935.

[9] *Lokavrittanukarana* (*Natya Sastra*, I, 110). The word *loka* has the diverse meanings of the English word "world": the universe in a general and rather vague sense; this or that particular cosmic system; the ensemble of sensible things; humanity and especially profane humanity, the natural society, "the people."

[10] The first performance created a scandal. The saint Bharata, obliged with his hundred sons to organize it, found nothing better to present than the victorious struggle of the Devas against the Asuras. The latter, invited to the spectacle, became enraged, and the battle on stage was extended to the performance hall itself. Brahma had to intervene and explain to the two enemy troupes that, in their antagonism, Devas and Asuras were indispensable to the harmony of the universe and, consequently, to that of the theater, which is an image of it.

[11] *Sahitya-darpana*, by Visvanatha Kaviraja. This work (fourteenth century A.D.?) most fully describes the school of *rasa* (of the "savor," see further on), and is, perhaps, the most profound of all treatises on poetic art, Hindu and otherwise. There is an English translation of it, very literal and difficult to read, by R. Ballantyne and Pramada Dasa Mitra (Bibliotheca Indica, Calcutta, 1875).

[12]*Sahitya-darpana*, I, 2. An allusion is made to the principal protagonists of the *Ramayana*.

[13]See P. Masson-Oursel, *Une connection entre l'esthétique et la philosophie de l'Inde, la notion de pramana*, in the *Revue des Arts Asiatiques*, 1925, and *L'Esthétique Indienne*, in *Revue de Metaphysique et de Morale*, 1936. See also A. K. Coomaraswamy, *Introduction to the Art of Eastern Asia*, Boston, 1932 and other works.

[14]I must say that in this phrase no Sanskrit word would be translated by "beautiful." The aesthetic value of a plastic work is expressed by its "conformity to pramana," that of a poetic work through its "richness in *rasa*." Apart from this, a quantity of terms (*sobha, saundarya*, etc.) designate the exterior and sensible "beauty" which can belong to natural objects as well as to works of art and which are, in the latter, only an incidental embellishment. One word, however, in the treatises on poetry, defined beauty psychologically: *samatkarita*, "the power to provoke supernatural admiration." (See further, the "savor.")

[15]*Samketa*, the thesis of the *Kavya-prakasa*, an important treatise of Mammatacharya (thirteenth or fourteenth century A.D.).

[16]Bhartrihari, one of the "jewels" from the court of the sun-king Vikamaditya (beginning of the fifth century A.D.?) is known, above all, for his *Centuries* of profane interest. But, an adept of the *Vedanta*, he also expounded the linguistic doctrine of the school in the *Vakyapadiya* ("Of the Phrase and the Word"), unfortunately unpublished in Europe.

[17]*Sphota* evokes the blossoming of a flower, the development of a bud—thus a constant germinative power hidden beneath the appearances which manifest it.

[18]Similarly, there are also two musics; one, *anahata*, "not produced by agitation," is the music of the gods and ancient *Rishis*; the other, *ahata*, is the music that is perceptible to the ear. And two kinds of dance and dramatic mimicry, etc.

[19]I cited many more details on this subject in *Measures*, April 1938. Here it is understood that we speak of the rhetorical and poetic uses of language only. In the liturgy and in the art of incantation, still other "powers" of language intervene: qualities of timbres, articulations, accents, meters, modes of recitation, etc., which depend on the science of *mantra*; the latter is reserved for a small number while poetry is accessible to all "who have a heart" (*sahridaya*). We do not speak of the Vedic poetry, fruit of a "nonhuman" art.

In the didactic texts, the Vedic glossaries, the commentaries to the sacred works, still another resource of language is employed. It is the *nirukta,* "explication of words," at which the Indologists like so much to jeer. Translating *nirukta* by "etymology," they play a good game, calling it "whimsical" etymology and seeing in it only pedantic puns. In fact, the *nirukta* does not presume to be a scientific "etymology"—if indeed a scientific etymology could exist. The *nirukta* "explains" a word by developing the meanings contained in its constituent parts and the verbal associations that could help the memory to retain its content and the diverse aspects of the idea that it signifies. Thus, the etymology of the word *Upanishad* from the root *sad,* "to sit"—"gathering of disciples seated at the feet of the master"—is "scientifically exact," but it teaches us much less than the "whimsical etymology" given by Sankara: "that which resolves completely, to the end (error)" (commentary to the *Katha Upanishad*). Similarly, the explication of *saman,* "liturgical chant," from *sa* ("she") + *ama* ("he"), developed at length in the *Chandogya Upanishad,* reminds the poet that by chanting he activates within himself a marriage between two forces, male and female; and elsewhere the same text gives, for the same word, a totally different explanation, thus refuting all question of "scientific etymology." This digression seemed necessary to underline the *spiritually practical* (and not intellectually discursive) value of the Hindu verbal elaborations.

[20]The adepts of the *Nyaya* accept yet another significant function, belonging no longer to separate words but to the whole of the phrase, to which it would assure a logical liaison. For our author, who follows the *Vedanta,* this function is indistinguishable from the act of discourse, it is identical with the intention of the speaker. The first thesis is a logician's view, the second that of a psychologist.

[21]An analysis of the *Sahitya-darpana* reveals 5,355 types of suggestions.

[22]Incomplete definitions, because they only enumerate the external characteristics of poetry (see further: qualities, ornaments) or indicate conditions which are necessary but not sufficient (such as the "harmony of words and meanings," Mammara, Bhamaha); others state that the function of suggestion characterizes poetry (*Dhvanyaloka, Kavyalocana*), but they do not say what is suggested. King Bhoja, the author of the *Vyaktiviveka,* also defines the essence of poetry as *rasa,* and this doctrine is certainly the richest in meaning.

[23]*Vakyam rasatmakam kavyam, Sahitya-darpana,* I, 3. The following citations: ibid., III, 33 sq.

[24] The comparison between poetic gustation and the gustation of a culinary preparation is developed in the sixth lesson of the *Natya Sastra* (see Subodh Chandra Mukerjee, *The Natya Sastra of Bharata*, chapter VI, *rasadhyaya*, thesis, Paris, 1926).

[25] *Pramatri*. This "capacity to judge," this interior measure, is, according to a commentary, "the result of merits from a previous existence." Beauty is relished only to the degree for which one has prepared oneself.

[26] The savor belongs neither to the poet nor to the auditor; neither to the actor nor to the spectator; but it unites them in a single moment of consciousness.

[27] Although the *rasa* is unique, in practice one distinguishes several "savors," according to the emotions which color it: Erotic, Comic, Furious, Pathetic, Heroic, Wondrous, Repugnant, Horrific, to which certain authors add Tranquility ("appeasement" of the emotions, attended by the desire for deliverance and related to religious love) and the Parental (maternal or paternal love).

[28] With other authors (like Dandin) the *guna* are hardly distinguishable from the "ornaments." I follow Visvanatha (S.D., VIII) who follows, here, Mammata. The same for the *riti* (S.D. IX).

[29] This is made possible by Sanskrit syntax, which can be more "analytic" or more "synthetic" according to whether it utilizes many or few long compound words. But each language can obtain the same effects with its own resources.

[30] I always say "auditor" and not "reader" because the silent read is never a substitute for the direct auditory experience; and even when one reads, one listens internally.

[31] There are seventy-nine principal ones in the *Sahitya-darpana*. Those of "sound" (alliterations, etc.), others of "meaning"; these last lead, for the most part, to explicit (*upama*) or implicit (*rupaka*, metaphor) comparison. The importance of the different methods of comparison strongly affects the character of the artistic process: a similar interior act establishes an analogic identity between phenomena of different natures. The "comparison" also exists in the plastic arts; the line of a woman's eye is similar to that of a siren's body, the torso of a man drawn like the head of a bull seen straight on, etc.

We note here that one of the great resources of our art, the imitation of nature, is for the Hindu only an *alamkara* which is of little importance and which must not be abused (No. 68 in the S.D.).

[32] The same for the musical, architectural, etc., ornaments.

[33] There are, nevertheless, certain correspondences between meters and *rasa*. The long syllables, in series, correspond to the pathetic, the repugnant; the short in rapid succession to the heroic, the furious, etc. ... (*Natya Sastra*, XVII, 99 et seq.). Sanskrit prosody differs little from Greco-Latin prosody. The meters are in fixed or variable numbers of syllables, in a quantity entirely or partially fixed. A cadenced prose, called "prose in the perfume of meter," also exists.

[34] *Agni Purana*, Text 336, stanzas 3 and 4.

[35] *Vishnu Purana*, cited in the *Sahitya-darpana*, I. An author on the *samgita* (the ensemble: chant-music-dance) says the same: "In serving musical sound one serves the gods Brahma, Vishnu, Siva, because they are, themselves, composed from it."

[36] The danced mime (*nritya*, superior to *nritta*, or imitative dance, and based on *natya*, or dramatic art) is, like poetry, an art which simultaneously animates distinct elements: rhythms related to music; emotions (*bhava*) expressed by the attitudes and methods of movement which support the *rasa*; and intellect, through a sequence of specific gestures (*kara*, really manual words, more commonly known as *mudra* in Buddhist sculpture or statuary).

According to the *Kavya-prakasa*, the conditions necessary to produce a poet are: 1) A natural aptitude (*sakti*), a certain internal "conformation" (*samskara*), without which there can only be a caricature of poetry; 2) a technical knowledge (*nipunata*) which is acquired by a study of the world, the sciences of language, the four "goals" of human life, the natural sciences, the great poems, etc. ... (Vamana, more ancient, cited, as well, the erotic science and the political art, to which he gives an important role); 3) exercises practiced in an assiduous manner under the direction of a master.

[37] *Vishnudharmottara-purana*, cited by P. Masson-Oursel, *L'Esthétique Indienne* (article cited), after J. Przyluski, *Danseur et musicien*, in the *Revue des Arts Asiatiques*, 1931, No. 2, p. 79.

ON INDIAN MUSIC*

"The musician of silence"
S. Mallarmé

I did not wish to hear the vocal din with which the French public, oppressed by too much unrecognized beauty, relieved itself after the gala premiere of Hindu dances and music given, but as one gives sweets to pigs, March 3, 1931, by Uday Shankar and Timir Baran Bhattacharya.[1] And yet, I was unable to stop my ears with enough alacrity to avoid hearing these few words with which the arthritic bourgeoisie publicly tickled its throat (an assuredly learned view): "The music of those people babbles, like their philosophy, always the same measure or the same proportion, for hours or for centuries, all the same monotone." I agree, madame, it's always the same object that compels that resonant music and philosophy: open your eyes before that which you actually are. Have you seen only a desert of boredom? Whose fault is this?

Man's great enemy, with whom he is engaged in a struggle to death, is time. Consciousness of pure time, void of content, is intolerable. Try, only for a moment, to concentrate on passing time and on nothing else. If you succeed, you are beyond all this. Occidental man seeks, through a myriad of means, *to kill time*, filling it with sensations, emotions, justifications, diverse agitations, or much more commonly, with automations that replace all this and permit him to sleep twenty-four hours a day, beneath the guise of a mechanical, more or less well-regulated human being. He invents calendars and watches to transform the merciless duration, compels

---

*First published in *La Nouvelle Revue Française*, 1931. Later reprinted in *L'Evidence absurde*, Paris, Éditions Gallimard.

his life to conform to a mathematical time, to an objective law of nature, exterior to himself, estranged from his intimate sensibility. And yet, these veils, eclipsing the reality of time, reveal themselves to be illusory and vain: duration resuscitates itself in the cruel form of *boredom*. The Oriental, and I speak of the Oriental who thinks,[2] in general has chosen another form of combat. He does not try to *kill time* with a thousand methods of sleep, that is to say, by killing himself. On the contrary, by living time, he identifies it with himself and annihilates it in his own consciousness. Thus, contrary to common prejudice, he knows better how to live and assimilate the immediate reality than the Occidental, who strains his ingenuity to flee by innumerable detours.

And then, all music silences itself in duration, measures duration; like duration, it is irreversible succession. Thus, the music, whatever else it may be, is concretized time; it is audible time. This precious vehicle permits us to grasp inaccessible time. It can be foreseen that both Oriental and Occidental man will utilize the art, each in his way, in order to contend with the old enemy. The contrast in their methods of combat can be discerned in the musical traditions of the two civilizations.

In fact, Oriental music bores all purely Occidental individuals. Instead of masking time, man's formidable devourer, beneath a beautiful sequence of sound, instead of *distracting* him, it incessantly recalls the gnawing obsession, it returns, it insists on intensifying the sorrowful consciousness of time. The Occidental seeks, in his approach to music, a sonorous procession that will clothe and conceal duration. The musicians of India, if not of the entire Orient, require from sound only that it manifest silence. Thus, said Lao-Tzu,[3] ten rays unite to form a wheel; but the void in the center allows the wheel to be used; and similarly, a vase is valued not by the breadth of its sides but by the void which they determine. The Oriental musician aspires, above all, to sculpt in the duration a sequence of *silent moments*; and the listener realizes each of these moments as the substance of his own life, of his consciousness, grieved to be limited, to be enclosed in an individual skin.

René Daumal

The word "to listen" has two very different meanings, depending on whether it refers to one or to the other of these musical expressions. The Occidental savors, in listening to music, a double pleasure, melodic and harmonic. At first, I will speak only of the melodic. In the most favorable situation, when the melody is not simply a base satisfaction of his instincts, his passions, stirred and pleasantly calmed by the power of sonorous sequences, that which he admires is principally the skillful resolution of a problem posed by the musician. The first measure brutally breaks the silence. *Fiat sonum*: The sound is separated from the silence; the equilibrium is broken; the melodic world with its laws is already sown in this initial measure. To complete his creative glory, the musician must develop this seed, to re-establish, after diverse events, diverse vicissitudes, the equilibrium of primitive silence. But, from the beginning, a law is imposed on the musical development; the first rupture of silence provokes a second, then a third, and so on. This display of creative power can, in the case of a genius, create all over the skin bristling granules of the sublime. Most often, I prefer to look coldly at the auditor, anxiously suspended in the melodic theme, asking himself, at each instant, how will the musician remove himself from the difficulty of his situation, and he sighs with an admiring satisfaction when, at last, the sequence of sonorous equations resolves itself in the final silence . . . Time has been conquered. The reality which is hidden behind the melody, to which his admiration is addressed, is that of an individual will powerful enough to impose itself on the passage of time.[4]

Asian man is unrelated to this art. Particularly for the Hindu, the melodic problems have been resolved for centuries. The individualism of the Western artist, who wants to surpass himself, realizing through his creation the image of a god who is personal to the work, has no reality for the Hindu. An ancient tradition has limited the number of musical themes—we might better say, to translate the untranslatable word *raga*, musical colorings. The technique of the *raga* is meticulously governed by very precise and complicated rules. Each *raga* is linked to an hour of the day, a season of the year, a state of being; it is male or female, it is this or that color. The *ragas* are also connected to precise mythological subjects; they are often represented, in the plastic arts, as living beings. (This does not astonish the Hindu mentality, for which the hymns, stanzas, and formulas of the *Vedas* have been *seen* by the ancient *Rishis*.) All this can disconcert the musician or simply the Occidental auditor. But he must hear the Hindu musician if he wants to comprehend the miraculous usage to which these traditional theories are applied.

He will then understand that the musician utilizes the *raga* somewhat as the poet utilizes words, fixed in specific grammatical form but developing through the skillfulness of his expression infinite networks of correspondences. And the *raga* has a much greater suppleness; with a single one of these themes that govern the ancient laws, the musician, by a subtly nuanced repetition, by an interlacing of the *raga* with himself, arrives at a realization of the true object of his art—the expression of moments of silence, to which the traditional themes give precise "coloration," permitting each listener to relish more concretely the savor of suffering. And each theme is universally, humanely simple: the night, the morning, the spring, the evening ... I understand that a Western man, a truly and purely Western man, cannot tolerate the feeling that he is nude and alone in an afternoon that is eternal, or in a first evening watch that will never end, that pitilessly returns, ten times a minute, in an eternity of boredom. But if, by an act of love, he identifies himself with the Hindu listener, with the music, with the musician himself, if he has the courage to affront his own solitude, he will hear, but with something other than his ear of flesh, a new unsuspected music.

Each measure returns to each instant of silence. In each silence, man finds himself once again alone, facing himself—and it is always the *same* moment. The duration, resolved in identical instants, spreads out in a unique act of consciousness. The individual comprehends himself, as he is, in the concrete present of an instant. Another melody is born: no longer from the succession of notes, but from the relations between these moments of silence. From this comes the feeling often noted by Occidentals of a music that develops according to a new dimension of time; a music that imposes its rule, no longer on the corporeal existence but on a more intimate order, a more subtle form of existence. It is also impossible to transcribe, with our system of notation, that which is the essence of the Hindu *raga*.

And the musical tradition of India insists that a given *raga* must allow the listener to grasp the naked reality of his immediate existence. The *raga* is thus a truth: it attains its full significance only when played in the hour for which it was conceived. Keyserling, an Occidental amateur interested in Orientalism, having visited Tagore's home to sample some Indian music, recounts, "When last night, on a desire that I expressed, someone played, on a winter's evening, a theme from the middle of summer, the musicians seemed at first, uneasy; this seemed impossible to them."[5] And the suggestive power of the music is such that, under its impulse, as under that of every source of living thought from India, the count-traveler-philosopher wrote several well-stated truths on the subtle art of *raga*. Hindu music, through its relation to concrete being, could accomplish that night, one more time, the real goal of the music, which is to provoke man to become conscious of himself.

The function of the instrumental ensemble for an Occidental and for an Oriental listener reveals the same contrast. Harmony, for the Occidental, is subjectively defined by its agreeable character. Agreeable because it pleases the body, pacifies the organs, and permits the passionate impulses to repose in the sleep of their repression. Harmony, then, is agreeable, that is to say, void of meaning. It assures to the listener a calm or a moderate and pleasing agitation of the instincts by giving, in a certain way, a body, a passionate substance, to the melody. The same man, if he listens to the dissonances of an Oriental orchestra, or, even more, to an orchestra of "primitives," is disagreeably troubled. He criticizes the concord as displeasing. He does not realize that the effect which troubles him, which disturbs him, is not the acoustical phenomena which are indifferent in themselves to all value judgment, to all affective appreciation. If he is stirred, it is by something within himself—in the depth of his being, a profound movement of the animal instinct, repressed for a long time by the training of his social life, now perhaps awakened. He would prefer not to acknowledge it; he has spent his entire life refusing to acknowledge it.

Hindu music here remains strictly faithful to the supreme device of γνῶθι σεαυτόν (*gnothi seauton*).[6] Knowingly, with a limited number of meticulously measured chords, which appear all the more strange and barbarous to the Occidental ear, it penetrates a man and transforms him completely. Harmony, in the restricted meaning of agreeable accord given to it by the Occidentals, plays a more or less nonexistent role in the Hindu orchestra, because its real meaning, as I have said, its power to awaken, is equally annulled. The living harmony of the music of India is the result of a simultaneity of rhythms, complex and precise in their interlacings, which mimic, marvelously, the endless multiplicity of a life; it triumphs when this wise diversity resolves itself suddenly in a final dissonance, a unique cry of the grieving consciousness, or in the positive silence that encloses a whole universe. The music of the Occident has lost this sense of primitive rhythms; it has forgotten that these rhythms can inspire thought. It subordinates the rhythm, simplified, denuded of its richness and efficacy, to the principal goal, which is to "distract," to "kill time."

The theme of the *raga*, in manipulating the thread of the duration of silent moments, imposes on the individual the void form of his immediate consciousness. The accords and the dissonance give content to this form; the organic being of man, with all its contrary and discordant tendencies, is finally awakened and placed in the only light in which it can be free—in the lucid consciousness of the instant.

All primitive people knew how to utilize the irresistible powers of certain rhythmic alliances, certain dissonances. Sometimes, by a very simple process, such as frenetic acceleration, they can augment still more this power to violate and dominate the human synesthesia. Thus music became one of their principal instruments of sorcery, magic, or social communion. The music of the Ibos of Nigeria, to take one example among thousands, "touches" the most intimate chords of the human being; it evokes his primitive instincts. It evokes for the individual a world so complete that, as long as it endures, his spirit is somewhat separated from his body.

Even the European, however limited his disposition for the music, is compelled to feel the elemental forces of his nature strangely moved by the passionate fervor of the possessed musicians.[7]

The magical music of the primitive inhabitants of India probably nourished the more civilized art of the Aryans. I could verify the almost hypnotic effect on myself that the Ceylonese Dravidians, however much they had adapted to the public of the great halls of Europe, obtained from several rudimentary percussive instruments. Probably when the Aryans penetrated the Sapta-Sindhu they discovered analogous musical practices in the Dravidians who were originally established there.

And thus, the Hindus, evolving from an extraordinary racial mixture, knew better than any other people how to master the magical power of music, disengaging it from religious ritual and channeling it, by a rigorous process of refinement, toward goals more precise and more detached than those of conjuring or propitiatory magic. Their rapid progress and soon their masterly fabrication of instruments permitted them to fulfill the task. Several of their instruments, such as the *sarod*, derived from the most archaic lute, are equipped with a large number of supplementary strings which uniquely serve the resonance; but due to the richness of the series of possible resonances, and to the suppleness of the instrument in the hands of the interpreter of the *raga*, this body of wood and strings, designating a schematic living being, vibrates and responds to each emitted note, while the listener, the human being, responds similarly, in silence. And from this derives a force of psychological penetration, the more profound because it is not related to the intensity of the sound. On the contrary, the Hindu musician knows how to play marvelously almost in silence; he plucks a string: living echoes awaken in the instrument as they simultaneously awaken in the audience. The spiderlike agility of his fingers then modulates, with precise palpitations, the luster of the resonances; he lets the sound die, sculpting it until its death, until silence. And we feel that he continues to sculpt the silence. At this moment, the music becomes almost *visible* around the musician; his fingers seem to be wielded by silent, luminous veins. The man who knows how to listen, in this supreme moment, finds that he has been awakened by a musical miracle, in an instant of perfect silence. The melody, which imposes the form, and the harmony, which evokes the living substance, are reunited in their common goal: the silent moment of the perception of the self.

The perfection of this art is related to the exceptional historic circumstances, too little noted, which one might call the *Hindu Miracle*, the origin of an entire civilization—as one refers to the "Greek Miracle" at the origin of our own. India, in contrast to Europe, while acceding to reflective thought to the point of having from antiquity a syllogistic and scholastic logic, did not forget the primitive foundation on which every civilization is built. Despite the Brahmans and their care to protect, through the caste system, the integrity of the white race, from the first centuries of the Aryan immigration a fertile interpenetration operated between the newcomers, the Dravidians and the more ancient aborigines. This co-existence, between two varying developments of the human mind, is evident in the Hindu writings; in the outlines of a perfectly logical and coherent doctrine, one notes, in a certain *Upanishad*, the manifestation of the inextinguished life of primitive magic. Likewise, the emotional power of primitive music is conserved in the Hindu system, but it is subjected to the most elevated function which can be given to an institution or a human art: that of awakening the consciousness, of provoking men to perceive themselves as they are.

It would be artificial to speak separately of Hindu music and dance. When Shankar dances, he is like the orchestra's principal musicians—a musician whose music would definitely have silenced itself. The *ragas* are replaced by *mudras*, gestures fixed by tradition, each having a signification as precise as a word and which, through their evocative power, can touch an Occidental who is ignorant, as I am, of their exact meaning. The musicians accompany the dancer, their gaze concentrated on his movement. They adroitly envelop him with their rhythms, as if to sustain his silent gestures. They support his dance, create in each instant the atmosphere within which the gesture can attain its full value. The dancer and musician are joined by a rigorous mathematical law; in fact, they do *the same thing*, exactly; we search for the invisible threads which unite them. The dance attains its moment of completion, signified by certain instances of immobility, gulfs of consciousness suddenly hollowed by the fixed gesture of a dancer and by the sudden simultaneous silence of the orchestra.

The usage of these *ragas* and *mudras*, subject to rigid secular laws and yet open to the free interpretation of the dancers and musicians, permits the extraordinary scope of Hindu mimicry. As actor and dancer are, in general, indistinguishable from each other, the mime can recount through his dance the most complicated legends, all of them familiar to the Hindu spectator. In the old danced drama, spoken language was even omitted. Extremely animated mimed dialogues were expressed by the actors while the orchestra enveloped the mimicry in the sonorous atmosphere which permitted its full development. At times, the orchestra transforms itself into a choir, and human voices rise to glorify the heroes. In spite of the attitude of the orthodox Brahmans, the people of all religious sects unite on the stage (to their greatest gratification) gods, kings, jinn, and demons from all the cults of India. The innumerable legends of Siva, Rama, and Krishna, the embellishments that animate the great epic poems, all the traditional subjects of folklore, sustained by the direct, irresistible power of the music, are thus capable of touching the people down to the most humble peasant. At the same time, to the literal meaning of the legend, to the affective meaning of the accompanying music, is added a spiritual drama, not symbolized but directly resuscitated in the consciousness, by that which I call, grossly I confess, the succession of moments of silence and immobility. The possibility for a man to experience this last level is in no way linked to the intellectual culture into which he was born; it depends entirely on the power of his consciousness.

It is to be feared that Shankar, his musicians, and dancers will be induced to make heartbreaking concessions to "good taste," sovereign of the French bourgeoisie. It is true: when, with seven or eight dozen Hindus in the audience and a dozen Occidentals not very proud to be so, I held my gaze fixed on Siva-Shankar brandishing, with an entirely evocative gesture, the imagined corpse of the demon-elephant Gajasur, it was very painful for me to hear twenty stomachs shaking on their seats, twenty imbeciles who saw one thing only, somewhat strange in fact: the actor, who until then, had taken the demon's role, became unnecessary; his death sufficiently visible in the precise gesture of Siva, he peacefully arose and returned, with his elephant head, to the wings. Since then, in a second performance,[8] the actor-elephant uselessly remained with his four paws on the carpet until the end of the performance; and I am convinced, it was less disagreeable than to hear the laughter of those amateurs of Orientalism, but it was false.

It is probable, alas, that in deference to this sacred public "taste," the future spectacles which will be presented here by Shankar, the dancer, and Bhattacharya, the musician, will no longer be what the first two were: as I cannot imagine what could be a better résumé, in a single evening, of the multiple possibilities of expression in Hindu music and dance mimicry from the popular dances—peasant dances of seeding and harvest; wedding or sword dances; the mimed legends of Indra, the master of the dance, and the Gandharvas, his celestial musicians; the pastoral dances of Krishna and Radha; the very beautiful sampling of old Hindu drama, the *Tandava Nritya*; the dance of Siva—to the most pure, skillful, and penetrating interpretations of the classical *ragas*, through which Timir Baran Bhattacharya and his musicians allowed a few Occidentals to suspect, for the first time perhaps, that infatuating reality which they did not want to experience: *time* and its essence, *silence*.

—1931

NOTES

[1] This article was published in the NRF on the occasion of the performances in Paris of Uday Shankar, with his troupe of dancers and musicians.

[2] Once and for all, I want to clarify that the Oriental of whom I speak is the conscious Oriental; he is so, particularly, when he affirms himself to be an enemy of Occidental imperialism and colonialism. And the Occidental, with whom I contrast him, is especially the bourgeois Occidental, doubly a victim of his traditions and dogmas, because he must not only submit to them but must strengthen them in order to maintain his power.

[3] *Tao Te Ching.*

[4] There were, among Occidental composers, those who pursued aesthetic aims which were essentially foreign to the mentality of their civilization. In this study, they are excluded from discussion. The last and greatest of them was J. S. Bach.

[5] Count Hermann de Keyserling, *The Travel Diary of a Philosopher,* London, Cape, 1925.

[6] Know yourself.

[7] G. T. Basen, *Among the Ibos of Nigeria,* cited by L. Lévy-Bruhl.

[8] After a tour in Germany, Italy, etc., Shankar gave a new performance in Paris on the 13th of May. There were several changes in the program, unfortunately—those I had foreseen. But when he magnificently repeated the dance of Indra before the silenced orchestra, resuscitating the entire musical ensemble by the rhythmic sounds of his ornaments, the public received this as a tour de force.

CONCERNING UDAY SHANKAR*

In recent years, something extraordinary occurred in various European cities—in Paris, twice in the spring of 1931 and a third time in May 1932; in Monte Carlo, in August 1932. It was this: Hindu thought, alive, authentic, in flesh and bone, in sound, gesture, and spirit, was presented here in our very midst. Nothing deformed it, which is a miracle: neither ignorant translators nor hypocritical interpreters, nor even the smallest shadow of minor Theosophists.

Man must live lest thought degenerate. In those moments, thought was expressed not in words but in human bodies, those of Uday Shankar and his colleagues, musicians and dancers.[1]

I hope they will perform in France again some day, and if, because of these lines, two or three human beings seize the rare opportunity to see and hear that miracle, my debt toward those unexpected poets (for once the word is not misplaced) will be a little less immense.

If our words were not so worn, I would have already said enough. But will people believe when I say *poets*? I would really like to say conscious creators of charms, men who possess supernatural means of expression and utilize them to speak of the spirit. Will people believe that these miracles can actually make us cry with shame, can make us blush before the "spectacles" to which we go out of habit, in order to "distract" ourselves?

But it is so; it is not a superficial enthusiasm that has deceived me for a year and a half. To those beings, bearers of the always new immemorial beauty, I can offer no more than a barbarian's salute. In their presence, I felt grotesque, ignorant, false. As I watched them, the word "civilization" pronounced itself within me, perhaps for the first time, without evoking anything odious.

The great miracle of the arts and sciences of the Orient was there, millennial, perpetually reborn: the rigorous determinism of a tradition, opening to awakened individuals, the door to a real liberation.

---

*First published in the book *Bharata*, Paris, Éditions Gallimard, 1970.

Crippled in the chaos of the Occident, without a connecting thread, I can only wish to play the necrologist-poet to an inimical culture. The Orient is still alive. If, by a miracle, it is not dragged into the Occicental suicide, it will still live and there will be men on the earth who can think. But the Occidental free-arbitrary-dualist individualist, the sad capitalist-colonialist-imperialist, fettered with the etiquette of his order—he is finished.

"Spectacles," "distractions," "diversions"—shame! Watch passively, withdraw, forget, evade yourself; turn away from the great question—this is the immoderate collective pleasure of millions of my contemporaries, every day, morning and evening.

Neither the dance nor the music of India exist to *distract*. On the contrary, they exist to focus man's gaze incessantly on the intolerable center of his solitude, on the problem, on the absurd but dazzling power—the only power; and on the need to refuse the sleep of the earth. Even when Hindu music is gay, tender, sweet, friendly, it is mercilessly so, it is truthfully so, it is always merciless and true; and if we barbarians understand it a little, we will bow our heads before these pure existences.

Certainly these men bring us only a small sample of what still survives from the conscious art of Asia. And yet, how miserable even this little (if I dare say it) renders the desperate attempts for renewal in the music, dance, and modern theater of the West.

I believe myself capable of summarizing, in a few words, a rather common European opinion on Oriental music, as stated in an article by M. Boris de Schloezer.[2]

Oriental music is essentially "magic," sympathetic magic, and a little bit satanic; it would make no appeal to the intelligence. The Oriental auditor submits passively to it, asking only to be bewitched; he experiences a rapture differing only slightly from the intoxication of hashish (*sic*). Occidental music, in contrast, is "antimagic," thus praiseworthy and good. It asks, above all, to be "understood."

René Daumal

But what does it mean to "understand" the music? For the first time, I find a simple response to this question, a response directly inspired by M. de Schloezer's article. True, it would hardly be accepted, even by Occidental musicians. But it invaluably indicates a profound tendency in many Occidental listeners. Occidental music can be "understood" because "it has succeeded in subordinating all its sonorous elements to the melody"; and the melody is precisely the intellectual, if not intelligible, element in the music.

I believe I can translate in more simple language: "to understand" the music, for the average Western listener, is to be able on leaving a concert to whistle the melodies he has heard.

Now I would like to hear someone affirm, honestly, that *by the fact alone* of retaining a melody he has really *understood* something, gained the intelligence within himself of a truth. I do not believe that anyone can answer this challenge.

How clear that becomes to someone who listens to Hindu musicians, who hears them often and sees them dance their music—for dance and music separate no more than eye and ear. How clear it becomes to someone who hears and sees them without prejudging what he will not understand! Despite my ignorance of musical theories, I think I have "understood" at least this.

Through a universal symbolism the music of India speaks to the total man, in his three aspects: the stomach, the throat, and the head (as the cosmos appeared in the form of earth, atmosphere, and sky).

To the stomach, which embodies the whole life of the organic reflexes, the whole biological mechanism: the timbres, the intensities, the gestures.

To the thorax, which feels and feels again, with all the modalities of suffering and pleasure, desire and aversion: the *ragas*, the series of notes, fixed by ancient tradition, which determine the character of the melody according to the hour and the cosmic circumstances in which the musician plays. Each *raga* is associated with an hour of the day and a nuance of mood; I say truly "nuance," as *raga* properly signifies "coloring."[3] Its role, unlike the Occidental melody, is not to compel us to experience this or that emotion with a dilettante's pleasure, differing only slightly from the theologian's "morose delight"; its role is to harmonize human feeling with the conditions of nature in a given moment. (The rigid attitudes of Western spectators greatly disturb Hindu musicians, who consider it unnatural to play a *raga*, intended for dawn, at ten o'clock in the evening; and this rule, which astonishes at first, is, if we reflect upon it, very apt.) *Raga* is thus a very beautiful instrument with which to regulate human passions (and it is without doubt that which has been called "sympathetic magic," "hashish," etc.).

To the head, which is the intelligence, there is the rhythm (*tala*). And the rhythm, manifested by the musician, is the intelligible essence of things. But as soon as the head grasps a truth, it must make this truth accessible to the other parts of man's totality: then there is comprehension. Thus the rhythm, primordial element of Oriental music, is a structured resonance which addresses itself simultaneously to the most hidden resources of flesh and desire and to the most lucid facets of the spirit.

Occidental music hardly acknowledges this third element. Granted, it is not exclusively melodic, no matter what M. de Schloezer thinks, and it seems to have become less and less so during the last few dozen years. But, in general, when it abandons melody, it is prone to fall into chaos or into a muscular and nervous massage, more or less skillful and violent; Stravinsky's music is a good example.

Because of the pre-eminence of rhythm, drums, always numerous and varied, are accorded first place among Oriental instruments. In the opinion of Hindus, they are also the most ancient and require an extraordinary knowledge and technique: half a human life is necessary to become a proficient player.

I will try to recall, in weak verbal reflection, several moments of comprehension imparted to me by these artists.

René Daumal

Timir Baran Bhattacharya, with his sarod, suddenly became a sonorous sun, radiating waves of resonant silence.

Even imbeciles are crushed. Only the silence of certain cathedrals speaks, at times, with such lucidity.

I would like to say in Latin: *musicus silet*. "Silere"—active verb. For the Occidental today, the word is obscured by the thing. The *thing*, can I say, the *cause*: the cause of sounds is silence, as the one, or the nonmultiple, is the cause of the multiple.

Amid the diversity of sounds, this music always signifies the indescribable and positive silence. Silence and solitude before a single thing, which *is*. Which *is*—not audible but listening through the sounds that endure. All men suffer from a self-evident solitude. This is why brains were crushed and shoulders heavy, as sound slowed down from a quarter of a second to a century, from a quarter of a tone to silence.

What drama is enacted between Vishnu Dass Shirali and T. B. Bhattacharya? Shirali is seated in the circle of his ten drums, tuned according to a Hindu division of the octave; Bhattacharya, with his two hands, animates the sarod on his knees. The *raga* is for the mood, "Suffering Caused by Another," and intended for the hour "After Midnight." A double fugal movement, but there is more than counterpoint, for two rhythms also conjoin, create a living harmony, separate, rejoin, silence themselves in a mute separation, and once more commune. Drama, for as each player follows the theme of the *raga*, he strains his ingenuity to complicate the other's play, and they also dance, with the head and eyes. Living music—in the process of birth.

In the middle of a sonorous stairway of vertigo, Shirali *finds the time*, between two precipitated notes, nonchalantly to arrange a drum, which had perhaps displaced itself by a hair's breadth.

On another plane, when I will leave the hall after a few moments of charms, two and a half hours will have elapsed. Chronometers do not explode in the spectator's pockets. The chronometers don't have time.

Uday Shankar, perfect and all-powerful master, governs some four hundred and fifty muscles of his body; each one does exactly what he wishes it to do, obeying the head only and ignoring the neighboring tissues.

"Indra teaches the dance to the inferior divinities." From his multiple ornaments, from the calm thunder of his feet against the soil to the precise rhythms contradicting and reconciling themselves, his body, alone, recreates the music. It is recorded that on one day he silenced the musicians and danced, while an entire ensemble rang and reverberated from his limbs.

When the last bell of a bracelet is absolutely silent, accentuating the definitive gesture of an arrested finger—the silence and the sudden motionless stillness is that of the sky above storms.

Shankar by visible gestures, T. B. Bhattacharya by music gestures, both seek to represent the celestial Gandharvas, singers and dancers. But don't they actually embody these divinities, these poets from the court of Indra, these two men who are no more than two living expressions of a single word?

Krishna (Shankara) dances with the guardian-of-the-cows (Sirnkie) before revealing himself as Vishnu. They dance like children of a nobler age, but sometimes their arms stop for a moment in the air, tracing sacred signs of flesh, and I tremble with the prescience of things to come: the army of the Pandavas on the field of the sons of Kuru, the hesitation of Arjuna and his charioteer, and suddenly, like a thunderbolt, Krishna.

When Kanek Lata dances beside the Ganga (her arms trace the water with gestures of ritual ablution) she recreates one of those apsara friezes that adorn the temples of India. (But I assure you, one pinches oneself to be sure one is not dreaming. One can scarcely believe the beauty.)

A certain rhythm belongs especially to demonic beings. I recognized it. It is very similar to that which children sing and dance when they wish to taunt. (You know it by instinct and oral tradition; for adults, in the West, know rhythms no better than they know children.)

Several instruments are specifically reserved for the demons. Their sounds, which we would call *false* in relation to our musical scales, are true, however, in relation to their object. Certain intervals and certain tones appear only in connection with the demons; and no one is fooled, everyone recognizes the demon even if his intelligence seeks to deny it.

One of these demonic instruments as if by chance has the same colored circles and the form, but larger, of our *diabolo*.

The Dance of the Dancer of the Worlds
From the beginning of the drama the centuries are obliterated.

The choir, with the voice of instruments as old as the *Vedas*, celebrates the divine couple Siva and Parvati, who suddenly appear, statuesque, in the middle of the stage, without our having seen them enter, without any machinery at all. In the same way they disappear, so simply that not one of our directors could imagine the process. Then the musicians announce the approach of Gajasura. His hurried steps precede him, until suddenly he is there, dancing demonically on the entire earth, represented by a few square meters of planks. After these preliminaries, the drama, which I will recount in detail, begins.

The choir and the actors conjoin sonorous rhythms and rhythmic gestures to form a single action. Each, according to his own voice, recites the narration.

Siva (Shankar) and the Gajasura (Devendra) oppose each other. Siva fights with his divine weapons: with the five elements, the winds and dust, the forces of earth, atmosphere, and sky, and also with the serpent of his arms, whose undulations pervade the air like a moral wind.

Sita (Sirnkie), his manifest power, the reservoir of his energy, stands inexhaustibly beside the combatants. Her divine husband has met the most redoubtable forces. Body to body, tremendous clashes follow—still on a few square planks.

The demon is overwhelmed. (But what mysterious act of love do I discern in this struggle to death?) The choir sings a penitential psalm.

The great prince dances his victory. He dances himself and the world—the total movement. By *mudras*, ancient gestures which are words, and for which I do not have the key, by flashes I distinguish what he is saying with his body: the seed that he contemplates with love and regret in his palm, the seed which he suddenly envelops with his voracious heart. Terrible, all that he abandons in order to return to the sleep that engendered the world. And Sita, in her extensive power, is she not this world itself? She, the expansive movement that emerges from Siva; she, the liquor of immortality which he drinks. Terrible and sweet in turn, and more and more quickly, the two faces of the god of the spirit alternate, until suddenly he is one only—to destroy my heart.

Then the sleep, eternal, lucid, without duration; as Sita dances her distress at having to endure the burden of a body.

The beauty of these musicians and dancers, of their instruments, their attitudes of sustained attention, of presence, of continual reality and also the just and *real* harmony of their costumes; the truth of all this, the complete absence of decor; the musical splendor which animates this evocative dance and music, exactly rendering the duration while signifying the eternal immobility; all this wonder—at times I still believe that I dreamed it, as one dreams of a very ancient country, of men more wise and beautiful, of a golden age.

—1932

René Daumal

NOTES

¹The recorded music of the Orient is subject to Occidental sabotage. I listened to some "Hindu" recordings, made by a Tagore-species, in the "Hindu Colleges" (probably funded by some Annie-Besant): one easily recognized a melody and a cadence more Hindu than anything else, but which seemed mechanical; the orchestra was composed of European instruments (constructed according to a very different division of the octave), and to expose the amateur, someone had written on the label, in magnificent devanagari characters: "piano and violin." Other records seemed authentically Hindu but of a secondary caliber. Therefore, mistrust phonographs as well as books when you want to know the Oriental sources.

²NRF, August 1932. This article is useful in that it very explicitly and precisely opposes an article which I had previously published in the same review.

³It seems nearly certain that *raga* (color) and *rajan* (Latin: *rex*, *regis*) come from the same Sanskrit root *raj*: to color, to be infatuated with, to be transported by—a king being a man in whom the instincts of the chest, warriorlike and ambitious, dominated but who had not mastered inwardly the power of the intellect.

THE ORIGIN OF THE THEATER OF BHARATA*

An Account of the First Founding of the Theater, According to Divine Transmission

Introduction

THE TEXT

Bharata's *Natya Sastra* is the oldest treatise of Hindu dramatic art. *Natya* means dance and mimed representation, but from its origin the Hindu theater was a total art. It is dance, mimicry, music, chant, poetry, architecture, mise-scène, and even painting. The *Natya Sastra* is, in all these matters, the first authority; it is traditional knowledge; it is even called the fifth *Veda*.

By traditional knowledge (*veda*, *vidya*), one implies a doctrinal body which develops the sense of the original gnosis without obscuring from view the ultimate goal, which is knowledge; this last term, indeed, is only to veil a hole in our heads; it is for each of us to fill. From metaphysics and dance to the training of elephants and mechanics, for the Hindu, all doctrinal bodies are linked by a common goal, call it deliverance, consciousness, or unification; in learning archery or grammar, one learns to know oneself.

The Hindus cared little for chronology. If they attribute a great antiquity to the *Natya Sastra*, they imply by this a spiritual proximity to the teaching of the *Vedas*. In fact, the collection is a compilation which extends over several centuries, and certain passages seem to have been altered or interpolated in a rather recent era. The major part of the book is certainly very ancient. All other treatises on dramatic art and poetry cite Bharata; he himself cites no one.

*First published in the book *Bharata*, Paris, Éditions Gallimard, 1970.

Bharata, in contrast to later authors who make ample use of the "classical example," cites no written text. The "theater" to which he refers is not the literary genre which abusively took this name; his theater is still action, exercise, and rite, much more than representation. The language, simple and concise, well worked, versified with a mnemonic goal and often scoring a direct hit, is devoid of the precious or baroque ornamentation of later Sanskrit; but the technical vocabulary abounds in Prakrit and Dravidian words. This suggests an ancient pre-Aryan theatrical tradition which may still exist in certain parts of South India. We note the Shaivite tendency of the *Natya Sastra* and the absence of any sign that it was written after the spread of Buddhism. The treatise seems to have been written later than the old epics and at least four or five centuries before the birth of Christ. This chronology is vague and perhaps unimportant.

The orally transmitted text was not written down until a rather recent period. I used, as a basis for my work, the Sanskrit text established by Joanny Crosse. It is the only European edition and has been very useful to the educated Hindus themselves. Unfortunately, even it is incomplete.

THE AUTHOR

The word *bharata* is used in the *Rig Veda* as an epithet for Agni (the god of fire). There, according to Paul Regnaud, it retains its etymologic meaning of "carrier" and designates the sacred fire as a carrier of the sacrificial offering—the "hundred sons" of Bharata, being a metaphor for the multiple flames of the hearth. According to others, the Vedic Bharata already had the value of a proper name and referred to one of the chiefs of the conquering tribes of India (anciently called "the land of Bharata"); the "fire-Bharata" being a particular worship practiced by the tribe or family of this chief. Finally, expressions such as "the coming of Bharata" were commonly used to designate a bard or an actor; whether this means that he came from the land of the Bharatas or that he was affiliated with the dramatic tradition of Bharata, we do not know. It is probable that by an etymologic crossing frequent in Sanskrit the words "Bharata, Bharatic" had preserved a vestige of their original meaning, the actor being elsewhere (*Sahitya-darpana*, etc.) defined as "he who *carries* (who assumes) the individual nature of the personage whom he plays"; he is the *carrier* of role and of the poetic "savor," as the fire is the "carrier" of the offering. In short, we note in the name of Bharata a mythic and symbolic etiquette, summarizing, most likely, the tradition of a particular school, but no journalist of the era has passed on to us the cigarette brand which Bharata preferred, nor his favorite sports, nor if he belonged to the Academy.

THE DOCTRINE

From among the divergent schools that base themselves on the authority of Bharata, or "Muni" as he is often called, the most comprehensive is that of the "savor" (or *rasa*). The doctrine is developed in the *Agni Purana*, in the treatises of Bhoja, in the *Dasa-rupa*, and most thoroughly in the *Sahitya-darpana* ("Mirror of Composition"), from which I have summarized the definitions which follow.

Savor. The essence of poetry (here understood as theater) is savor (*rasa*). Savor is the immediate interior perception of a moment or a particular state of existence provoked by the functioning of the methods of artistic expression. It is neither an object, nor an emotion, nor a concept; it is an immediate experience, a gustation of life, a pure joy, which relishes its own essence as it communes with the "other"—the actor or poet. The savor is differentiated according to states or modes of existence (*bhavas*) of which it is the "supernatural" and disinterested perception. Technically, eight or ten "savors" are enumerated. They are named, metaphorically, after the emotions or rather the psychophysiological operations (*bhavas*) of which they are the intuitive ideas: erotic, comic, pathetic, furious, heroic, horrific, repugnant, wondrous; to which certain authors add familial and tranquil. Each poetic work must assert a dominant savor; the "mixed" savors characterize inferior genres only.

Manifestation. The word *bhava* (emotion, general state) also designates the ensemble of manifestations for each of these savors. There are therefore eight or ten permanent manifestations, constant for a work or a given person; they are defined by the use of this or that means of expression (see below); they "manifest" the savor for the sense at the same time that they evoke it within the spectator. Thirty-three transitory manifestations express all the emotions and incidental psychic states which vary and give nuances to the fundamental savor, and finally eight or ten voracious manifestations (such as tears, laughter, perspiration) express the dominating emotion when it becomes potent enough to subject man to physiological actions which, according to theatrical convention, supply indubitable signs of the actor's interior state.

Means of expression. The interior state is manifested by four principal means (*abhinayas*): gesture, voice, costume and decor, and corporeal expressions. (Music and chant are regarded as aspects of voice.)

Styles. There are four dramatic styles (*vritti*, literally, "appearance, manner of doing"): the "verbal style," in which words play the dominant role, suitable for religious subjects and tranquil moods; the "heroic" style, suitable to warlike subjects and epic events; the style of the "coiffure," the name of which is taken from Vishnu's hand movement when he retied his hair after combat, suitable to the pathos of love; and the "fantastic" or "violent" style, in which the diverse mechanical artifices conjoin, suitable to magical drama and violent, supernatural combat.

The concepts of savor, manifestations, expressive means, style, and still others were enumerated, subdivided, numbered, labeled with the names of divinities, and carefully classified by the Hindu theoreticians. These classifications have a definite mnemonic value and are particularly adapted to oral instruction. The poet or actor who masters them can by a single glance of his inner eye embrace and animate all the potentials of his profession. And all that "knowledge," fastidious and complicated in appearance only, has no other aim than to liberate the artist from the poverty of his individual fantasies.

René Daumal

THE TRANSLATION

Up to the present, no one has translated the *Natya Sastra* into a European language, except for some of its most technical and, for the Occident, least relevant chapters. (See Sylvian Levi, in *Le Theater Indien*. His only endeavor, however, was to reveal the "pious credibility" of the Indian—but he added, the European will not know how to "enjoy it.") I read and attempted to translate this text in a completely different spirit, thinking, in the Oriental manner, that a text is made to serve man, not to enslave him. I have thus attempted to extract the maximum meaning, not hesitating to give full etymological value to certain expressions whose significance has certainly been weakened for the Hindu reader of today. The problem involved in the translation of mythological terms is nearly impossible to solve, its solution depending on the understanding and associations of each reader. I have indicated in the notes each particular term, always citing the Sanskrit word. Unfortunately, we do not have the commentary of Abhinavagupta[1] for the first chapters of the text.[2]

---

[1] A Kashmiri Shaivite of the eighth century, known for his mystical attainment and his commentaries on Sanskrit aesthetics texts.

[2] Since Daumal wrote this essay, the commentary of Abhinavagupta has been translated into English by Raniero Gnoli: *The Aesthetic Experience According to Abhinavagupta*, Varanasi, India, The Chowkhamba Sanskrit Studies, Volume LXII, 1971—LLL.

RASA or Knowledge of the Self

A Translation of the Natya Sastra
(The notes for the words with asterisks
will be found at the end of the translation.)

1. Bowing my head to the celestial great father* and to the celestial prince, I shall expound the teaching of the theater, which was articulated by Brahma.

2. Having finished his prayer* and being fixed in this vow, Bharata, the expert in the dramatic science was, on a day when studies were suspended, surrounded by his sons.

3. The hermits* came to sit beside him, sons of the devourer in front. And they, great in essence, masters of their thoughts and senses, questioned him:

4. "This work, this knowledge of the theater, perfectly attuned by the blissful one* to the measures of sacred knowledge, O priest: how did it arise and what was its cause?

5. "How many members does it have? What *are* its measures?* In which form is it used? O blissful one we beg you to tell us all these things as they are."

6. To these words of the hermits, the hermit Bharata responded with this discourse which is the history of the knowledge of the theater:

(*The recitation of Bharata:*)

7. May your presences become clear,* may you collect your thoughts, to hear the birth of the knowledge of the theater, product of the divine word.

8. Long ago, the age of perfection* and the reign of the son of the being born from himself were complete. Then came the

age of the number three and the reign of the thinker, son of the radiant sun.

9. And then there arose the profane law of the sexes.* Falling into the enslavement of desire and greed, misled by envy, anger, and all of the follies, the world was subject to pleasure and pain.

10. At that time, gods, titans, celestial musicians, specters, giants, and dragons* ruled the continent of Jambu, residence of the guardians of the world.

11. Through the voice of Indra, their prince, the gods said to Brahma, the great father: "We want something to delight us, something to see and to hear!

12. "The commerce* of the sacred knowledge cannot be communicated to the servile generations. Extract from it, therefore, a new and fifth knowledge, suitable for all of the castes."

13. "So be it," the great father said to them, and dismissing the king of the gods,* he rethought the four knowledges, rooting himself in his own unity—he who sees things as they are.

14. "The laws of justice, wealth, and glory,* with their practical exposition and presentation, the representation, for the worlds to come, of all forms of activity;

15. "the substance of all sciences, the activity of all professions —from all this and from the myths,* I make the fifth knowledge which shall be called the theater."

16. Thus the blessed one rethought the knowledges; and then the great father made the knowledge of the theater, product of the four members* of knowledge.

17. He drew recitation from the knowledge of the stanzas and chant from the book of melodies; mimicry was drawn from the knowledge of the rites and the savors from the book of the fire guardian.*

RASA or Knowledge of the Self

18. Thus, attuned by the great in essence* to the knowledges and to the secondary sciences, the knowledge of the theater was articulated by the blessed one, the omniscient Brahma.

19. Having produced the knowledge of the theater, the great father said to Indra, the powerful:*

"These myths which I have generated within myself must be transmitted to the gods.

20. "You must communicate this sacred knowledge called the theater to skillful beings,* beyond the fire of knowledge, who walk with daring and who have conquered inertia."

21. To these words uttered by Brahma, Indra, the powerful, joining his hands and bowing,* replied to the great father:

22. "The undisguised truth is that the gods, O blessed one, are not capable of grasping, retaining, understanding, and animating this science. They cannot be entrusted with the tasks of the theater.

23. "But there are prophets* who know the mysteries of knowledge, who have perfected their vows; they will be able to grasp, apply, and keep this teaching in their memories."

24. Having heard the words of Indra, the powerful, the being born from the flower of the waters,* said to me: "You, with the hundred sons that have been given to you, promote this theater, O you without agony!"

25. And thus commanded by the great father, I received the vision of dramatic knowledge; and I accurately taught its exercises and its practices to my sons:*

26-38. (In this section the one hundred sons of Bharata* are enumerated.)

39. At first, I instructed my one hundred sons; and I precisely divided the field of work, harnessing each son to the task which suited his aptitudes.

40. I used the verbal, heroic, and fantastic styles* to animate the dramatic action whose creation was my task, O two times born.*

41. But then the ancient of gods said to me:

"Use the gracious style and express the substance that it can convey, O best of the two times born."*

42. The eminent being thus spoke to me and I replied:

"O blessed one, may we be given and taught the useful substance of the gracious style!"*

43. In the soft movement of the limbs of the dancing god,* of the pacifier, I see with its essential savors, modes, and gestures,

44. the gracious style, clothed in tenderness, product of the erotic, but which men cannot practice without the concourse of feminine beings.*

45. Then the great hearth of force,* the everywhere radiating engendered with his thought the nymphs of the celestial waters—experts in the figures of the dramatic art, knowing the practice of the theater. They were manifested by the ancient one:

46. Fulgurant, Celestial Gift, Celestial Army, Very Judicious, Perfumed, Beautiful, Perspicacious, Clairvoyant,

47. Joy, Abundance, Russet, Good Humor, Soft Hair, Beautiful Coiffure, Varied Coiffure,

48. Mountebank, Silvery, Upright, Mane, Intoxicating, Beautiful Joy, Beautiful Face, and Nonarable,* and he presented them to me.

49. Swati* with her troupe of pupils was entrusted with the instrumental music, and the celestial musicians, directed by Narada, were entrusted with the vocal music.

50. Thus, aided by all my sons and directly assisted by Swati and Narada, I conceive this theater in its totality, adhering to the principles of the knowledge and its annexed sciences.*

51. I presented myself to the master of the world* to request his instructions regarding the drama to present, and, joining my hands, I said to him:
"We have received and grasped the science of the theater. Tell me now: what should be done?"

52. To these words, the great father answered:
"A great crowd has assembled to witness the drama;

53. "it is the time of the festival of the flag,* glorious festival of Indra, the great. Here and now you must animate this sacred knowledge entitled the theater."

54. Then, for the festival of the flag and the massacre of the titans* and the sons of the separated, to the crowd vibrant with immortals, on the triumphal day of the great Indra,

55. I presented first the benediction,* composed of propitious words, articulated in eight parts, grand and conforming to the sacred measures.

56. And then I presented the prologue, showing how the sons of the end* were vanquished by the gods—the provocation, the outbreak of conflict, the schism, the dissensions, and the battle.

57. Then Brahma and the gods, overcome with delight by this spectacle, radiant in spirit, came to offer us their services.

58. Indra, the joyous, the powerful, first offered his supreme standard,* Brahma offered his ewer, the enveloping one his golden vase;

59. the sun a parasol, Siva the magical vehicle, the wind a fan, Vishnu a throne of lions, the deformed one a diadem; and the celestial one river word* gave the sonorous substance of the spectacle.

60. All the others, gods, celestial musicians, specters, giants, dragons,* transported with joy by this seance, according to the diverse attributes of their natures,

61. offered their particular gifts, and they gave dialects, moods, savors, forms and forces, jewels and ornaments.*

62. But seeing the destruction of the sons of the bound and the sons of the separated thus represented, the sons of the bound who were present were scandalized.

63. And, turning toward the troupes of the hinderers,* led by the eye-deformed, they rose up and said:
"We cannot endure this theater. Let's attack!"

64. Thereupon, assisted by the other titans, the hinderers resorted to sorcery and paralyzed the words, the gestures, and the memory of the actors.*

65. Seeing this offense to the thread-bearer,* the king of the gods said to himself: "What has caused the play to cease?" and he rooted* himself in his thought;

66. he saw the hall beleaguered from one end to the other by the hinderers, the thread-bearer unconscious and immobile, and all the others in the same condition.

67. He arose with a furious leap, seized his celestial standard*— its gems flaming on the staff. He concentrated his gaze for an instant

68. on the hinderers and titans who were invading the stage, and then he sprang forward, the king of the gods, and with piercing blows he pierced their bodies.

RASA or Knowledge of the Self

69. Hinderers and sons of the separated, slain, the guests of the sky burst into laughter and said these words:

70. "Bravo! You won the celestial battle, you pierced the bodies of the sons of the separated.

71. "And, as the hinderers and titans were pierced by this standard, from now on 'pierced' will be its name.

72. "If the remaining hinderers rise again to impede us, they will see 'pierced' and quickly disappear."*

73. "So be it," said the powerful to the gods. "'Pierced' will protect you all."

74. Then, an even more elaborate entertainment was prepared for the powerful, but the spectacle had hardly been announced when the surviving hinderers incited a new fear in the actors.

75. Seeing this obstinate maleficence in the songs of the bound, I presented myself to Brahma, accompanied by my sons:

76. "Blessed one, the hinderers are sworn to the theater's destruction. Promulgate a law of perfect protection, prince of gods!"

77. Then Brahma said to the artisan of all:* "Make a house for the theater according to canonical laws, O great intelligence!"

78. And, without delay, the artisan of all made a large, light hall, conforming to all the canonical figures.

79. Hands joined, he went to the court of the striker,* and said to him: "The hall of the theater is ready, lord, lower your gaze to it."

80. Then, with Indra, the great, and all the other gods, the striker hastened to see the temple of the theater.

81. Having seen the house of the theater, Brahma said to the celestials: "Each of you, with your particular portion of being, must become a guardian of this temple of the theater."

82. The star of the months* was appointed to the protection of the surrounding walls, the four guardians of the world to their cardinal points, and the impetuous winds to the intermediary points.

83. Friend* sun was adjoined to the backstage, the enveloping one to the costumes, the fire messenger to the altar, and the guests of the sky to the orchestra.

84. The four castes were appointed to the pillars; the sons of the infinite and howling winds to the intervals between the pillars.

85. The phantoms were placed at the supports, the celestial nymphs in the halls, and the female specters in each of the rooms; the ocean, great vase of the waters, protected the soil, broad back of the earth.

86. The terminator* and the destroyer, time, were placed at the upright doors; two dragons, chiefs of colossal force, were posted before them.

87. The judiciary scepter was placed at the threshold, above it the pike of Siva; at the door two sentinels: destiny and death.*

88. Great Indra camped very near to the stage; the exterminator of the sons of the bound was the guardian of the dais.

89. Phantoms, specters, and subterranean colossuses surrounded the pillars of the dais.

90. The thunderbolt who slew the sons of the separated was appointed to the standard called "pierced"; the celestial princes of limitless forces to the knots of its staff:

91. Brahma, to the head of the staff, the pacifier, to the second knot, the blessed one Vishnu, to the third, the bounding* to the fourth,

92. and to the fifth the three great dragons: Sesha, Vasuki, and Takshaka.* Thus the gods, for the perdition of the hinderers, settled into and protected the standard "pierced."

93. Brahma camped in the middle of the stage; this is why we throw flowers onto the stage.

94. And the inhabitants of the abyss, specters, gnomes, and dragons, were installed as guardians under the stage.

95. The hero of the drama is protected by Indra, the heroine by the river word, the buffoon by the sound *aum* (the holiest of sounds), the other roles by the ravisher.*

96. "All these divine forces, installed here as guardians, are to be the tutelary dieties of this domain," said the eminent being.*

97. Then, the assembled gods said to the great father: "May you now, by your words, reconcile these hinderers.

98. "For it is ordained that one first seek a reconciliation, second that one give gifts; these methods failing, one attempts dissension; after which one resorts to the rod."*

99. Having heard this discussion of the gods, Brahma said to the hinderers: "Why did you come with the intention to destroy the theater?"

100. To these words of Brahma, the eye-deformed answered with this discourse which was the beginning of the negotiations with the sons of the bound and the troops of the hinderers:

101. "The knowledge of the theater, articulated by you, lord, in order to please the gods, was meant to teach us a lesson—you created it for the gods.

102. "Great father of the worlds, this was not a thing for you to do, for we, the sons of the bound, as well as the celestials, have come from you."

103. To these words of the eye-deformed, Brahma replied: "Enough of your resentments, sons of the bound, abandon your stupidity.

104. "You and the gods are joined through the opposition of good and evil;* according to this law and to the chain of actions and states of being, I have made the theater.

105. "Neither your nature nor that of the gods is exclusively represented by the theater; for it describes the manifestations of the triple world* in its entirety.

106. "Sometimes law, sometimes play, sometimes wealth, sometimes quiet, sometimes laughter, sometimes warfare, sometimes passion, sometimes violent death.

107. "Law for those who follow the law,* passion for those who are dedicated to passion, discipline for those who conduct themselves poorly, mastery for those who know how to proceed.

108. "To eunuchs it gives audacity and to braggarts, energy; it is the awakening of the erudites' unconscious and their perspicuity.

109. "Pastime of great lords, repose for the miserable, wealth for those who live by wealth, comfort for tremulous spirits,

110. clothed in the diverse manifestations* of life, incarnating the diverse phases of action, I made this theater conform to the action of the world.

111. "It is a receptacle of activity, for superior, inferior, and average men; it engenders useful teachings, and, from moments of tension to those of relaxation, it renders all joys.

112. "Thus through the savors, moods, and all modes of action this theater will be a source of teachings for all.

113. "The theater offers a refuge for those who are burdened with misfortune, labors, griefs or burned by an interior fire. For all, the theater will offer a refuge in this life.

114. "Showing the ways of law, glory, long life, and grace, fortifying the intelligence, this theater will be a source of teaching for the entire world.

115. "There is no understanding, no profession, no science, no art, no form of activity nor method that will not be presented in this theater.

116. "Therefore you have no reason to be resentful of the immortals; I have made this theater in the image of the seven continents.*

117. "Know that the theater represents the complete actions of gods and titans, kings and men, and prophets of the sacred word.

118. "All individual natures in the world, with their particular mixture of happiness and unhappiness, presented through corporeal mimicry and other means of expression: this will be called theater.

119. "To the sacred knowledge, to science and to myth, it will provide an audience, to the crowd a diversion: such will be the theater."

120. Then the great father said to the assembled gods, "Make a ritual sacrifice in this temple of the theater.

121. "May the offering consist of presents, fire libations, prayers, plants, and alms of food and drink.

122. "Entering the world of mortals, you will receive a luminous worship,* but no one must organize a spectacle without having performed the worship of the theater.

123. "Whoever organizes a spectacle, without having worshiped the theater, this one's knowledge will remain without fruit. He will be reborn in the womb of a beast.*

124. "The worship to the deities of the theater would, in fact, be a sacrifice. It must be accomplished with absolute concentration by those who are producing the performance.

125. "The actor or the head of the troupe who does not enact this worship or who does not have it enacted by his subordinates will only obtain defilement.

126. "He who performs the worship, according to the rite and with true understanding, will obtain the treasures of light and he will go to the world of the Solar Way."*

127. Having thus addressed the gods and the celestial powers, the striker gave this order to me: "Begin to worship the theater!"

RASA or Knowledge of the Self

Notes on the Translation of the Natya Sastra
(The numbers refer to stanzas in the dramatic text.)

1. "Great Father" = Brahma. "Prince" = Siva. The master of the word and the master of the dance are the fathers of the dramatic art. If you wish to translate "Brahma" say "the Speaker."

2. "Prayer" is an interior recitation of the *Veda*, accompanied by a very erudite gymnastic, in particular, certain dissociative operations of the text which aid in the realization of its inexpressed meaning. The "vow" is the choice, made by an individual, to fulfill his duty and to live according to his chosen discipline. The "suspension of studies" or interdiction from reading the *Veda* was enforced on certain days and in certain meteorological circumstances. (See *Laws of Manu*, IV, 101 to 128.)

3. The Sanskrit term *muni* (hermit) indicates a "silent" or "solitary" person. The *munis* concentrated their silences and solitudes around a master. The theater served the same function for the hermits of Bharata that music did for the Pythagoreans. The story which follows is supposed to have taken place among the "gods"; but it could easily be placed in the setting of an ascetic school, whose master would be Brahma. ("Brahma" also designates the person whose presence is necessary at every sacred process.) The *devourer* (Atri), like "bharata," is a Vedic name for fire. Atri is the son of Brahma; he engendered the moon with a single gaze. The descendants of Atri form a spiritual lineage which was probably linked to worship of Siva, as he sometimes is called "Son of Atri." "Great in essence" translates *mahatma*, which (if it carried its full etymological value) would accurately be rendered by "magnanimous."

4. "Blissful one," epithet of Brahma, translates *bhagavant* and implies the plenitude of his happiness and dispensatory authority. I use knowledge, sacred knowledge for the word *Veda*. "Priest" renders, rather inadequately, the word *brahma*, and in this context refers to Bharata himself.

5. "Its measures" would relate not only to the dimensions of the work but also the canonical rules which link a particular art to the original tradition and ultimately to the human being; when considered as a critic of art, he is called a "measurer" (*pramatri*). One notes that the term blissful one (as previously the term *Brahma*) changes in a few stanzas from a metaphysical principle to a human instructor, underlining the analogy between the "sky" and the school of hermits.

7. The expression "your Presences" is equivalent to a third-person term of politeness, and for "become clear" one would ordinarily translate "purify themselves." The notion of "purity" seems very vague, while the meaning of "clearness" applied to a personal "presence" is implied by the situation. In any case, it is the only meaning relevant to you and me, and I hope that you will follow the injunction of Bharata before continuing your reading. *Brahma* (in the neuter: the sacred word, the *Veda*, the absolute principle) is translated by the *divine word*, but one could also read "produced by Brahma" (in the masculine).

8. The names of the four ages (*yugas*) which constitute a complete cycle of humanity are taken from a game of dice (from the four marked faces or from four dice with individual marks): first, *krita*, "made, perfect" is the name of "4" in dice and that of the first age, also called the "age of truth"; second, *treta* is the "3" in dice and the second *yuga*; the Hindus also relate this word to the root *trai*, "to save, to conserve"; third, *dvapara* is the "2" in dice and the third *yuga*; fourth, *kali*, the name of the present *yuga*, signifies "black" or "black point"; it is the ace, the weakest point in the dice (it is the "4" which carries the stake, by its "virtue" which others would call Pythagorean). The relative durations of these four ages are like 4, 3, 2, 1. According to the *Laws of Manu* (I, 64), a thousand cycles of the four *yugas* form a "day of Brahma," in the course of which fourteen thinkers (*manu* = thinker or man) succeed each other as administrators of the creation. Bharata diverges somewhat from the usual conception in making the origin of the reign of *manu* correspond to the origin of the *treta-yuga*.

9. "Of the sexes" is a paraphrase which asserts itself. Literally, the expression is "the law of the village," that is to say, the law of the profane world, as opposed to the "law of the forest" or the ascetic life; in our time it signifies licentious sexual life. The event to which reference is made is the separation of the sexes which began in the *kali-yuga*. It may also signify the social (and consequently psychological) separation of man and woman. One notes that the presence of women, exceptional in the rites of worship and instruction, was, in fact, necessary to the theater; one of the aims, therefore, of the theater was to give women and the inferior castes (see stanza 12) access to the sacred instruction.

10. The translation of the names is based on the approximate mythological correspondences (and not on the etymology). Descriptions of these beings may be found in any Asiatic mythology. The Sanskrit names are *deva, danava, gandharva, yaksha*, and *mahoraga*. The "continent of Jambu" is one of the seven parts of the world; it can be: the human world,

the civilized world, Hindustan, or our planet. The name is derived from a fruit tree called the *jambosier*. The "guardians of the world" are the tutelary divinities of the parts of the world, the spatial directions, the diverse natural kingdoms, etc.

12. "Commerce" means the transmission of the *Veda* (from the mouth to the ear) reserved for the three "regenerated" castes (priest, warrior, peasant) who are the mouth, arms, and legs of universal man (*Rig Veda*, X, 91); the *Sudra*, the servile man, is said to be born beneath the feet of man; he does not directly participate in his substance. But the old symbol of castes, denoting specific functions of the human being, degenerated into an external social system. The *Sudra* proliferated, he had his own existence, he craved spiritual nourishment. Deprived of the long and indispensable preparation, he was unable to study the sacred science. It was necessary to create a special path for him. The theater was, thus, an effort to depart from a necessary esoterism; it was to be a work of communion which would address itself to all members of society, or, if you wish, to all of your corporeal members.

13. "King of the gods" = Indra. "Rooting himself in his own unity," literally, "resorting to *yoga*."

14. Justice, wealth, and glory are cited as three kinds of motives for human conduct. The usual explanation of these motives is: justice, intellectual desire for the good and true; wealth, desire for that which is necessary for the physical subsistence of oneself and one's family; passion, understood in a broad sense as the satisfaction of desires and emotions, the desire for beauty. The fourth goal, implied when it is not named, is deliverance, which consists in "renouncing, through a perception of their true value, the fruits of these first three desires" (*Sahitya-darpana*). "The worlds to come," although the expression is obscure, alludes to the new conditions of life which humanity will encounter in the *kali-yuga*.

15. The myths or, more literally, the "there was once upon a time"(*itihasa*) are the fables and epics which, with the *Puranas*, form the poetic investiture of the tradition. In the very ancient texts (see *Chandogya Upanishad*, VII, I, 1) these two collections form a "fifth *Veda*"; but it is the theater which will animate and give efficacy to this mythology.

16. These four members are: 1) *Rig Veda*, compilation of rhymed stanzas; 2) *Yajur Veda*, compilation of formulas and indications of ritual gestures; 3) *Sama Veda*, compilation of chanted hymns; and finally 4) *Atharva Veda*, a compilation of magic recipes, conjurations, and precepts for the protection of ritual processes.

17. I use book of the fire guardian for *Atharva Veda* because *Atharva* is known as the first priest of the fire. The aesthetic gustation is comparable to an illumination of thought. This is, perhaps, one of the reasons why savor is associated with the *Atharva Veda*. Another possible reason is that the fourth *Veda* applies, more specifically than the others, to the biological and social life of man and that savor is always an immediate gustation of a particular vital state. The *Vedas* are called "without savors" (*Sahitya-darpana*, I), and, in fact, the three original *Vedas* are free from particular psychological savors. But the *Atharva*, more related to individual life, does make use of the savors: for example, "the furious," in the imprecatory parts of the text.

18. "Great in essence" (see note 3) designates, in this context, Brahma. There are four secondary sciences or practical applications of the *Veda*: medicine, military science, music, and architecture.

19. "The powerful" (*sakra*) = Indra. Both myths and the theater are revealed by Brahma, but myth is the purely oral aspect of the new teaching, and the gods, who live in a world of pure sound, as they actually are engendered and nourished by man's words and chants, would be most apt to receive it.

20. These beings who, instead of possessing wisdom which is natural (and thus without merit), like the gods have acquired it by their activity, their intellectual ardor, their courage, and their asceticism. Brahma gives Indra the task of finding out who they are.

21. Indra makes the salute called *anjali*, which is still commonly used among the Hindus.

23. The *Rishi* (I use prophet in the Biblical sense) is "he who sees the hymns," who has the intellectual vision of the meaning of sacred words, and who transmits them to posterity. Expressions such as "mysteries of the *Veda*" are frequently used to designate the *Upanishads* whose fundamental instruction is to restore traditional knowledge to the individual consciousness (*atman* or *purusha*). The term "to understand" is not repeated in this stanza, but it is implied in the totality of the three operations of absorption, assimilation, and utilization of spiritual food.

24. Brahma is said to have "risen from the flower born of the water," that is to say, from the lotus, an image of diversity in unity. *Agha* or *anghas* is certainly agony or anger and not "sin" as it is ordinarily translated.

25. Brahma gives the science to Bharata, who teaches it to his sons; thus, all sacred science is transmitted, at first by direct vision and then by word.

RASA or Knowledge of the Self

From the beginning, the theater had its school exercises and its practice in public, but it was, above all, for the actor.

26. The translations of these names have a picturesque interest. They are, for the most part, the names of *Rishis* (teachers) known in the Vedic tradition, e.g., Sandilya ("descendant of the burning bull"?), Gautama ("descendant of the best of the bullocks"); or the patronymics of the epic heroes, e.g., Vatsya ("descendant of the calf"). Some names indicate a physical particularity (long members, bristled hair) or a moral (stupid, generous) or a function (umbrella carrier). In addition, one finds the names of elements and the names of animate or inanimate beings (water, swan, tamarind), etc. And finally, some technical terms of dramatic language (the horrific, the repugnant). It is possible that this list, varying elsewhere according to the manuscripts, was formerly a key (as often happens in this genre of mnemonic treatise). Here the absence of commentary is particularly regrettable.

40. On the four forms of dramatic styles, see the introduction. "Two times born" (*dvijas*) denotes members of the first three castes who have received the initiation.

41. Thus Bharata hesitates to introduce the erotic, feminine elements which were doubtless regarded with suspicion in the discipline of the school. "Best of the two times born" denotes members of the first three castes who have received the initiation, especially the Brahmans. Brahma is called here "*guru* of the gods"; *guru* means heavy, venerable and father or spiritual master.

42. One can also derive from the text a sentence which approximates to this: Could you extract from the gracious form all that is necessary in order to fornicate? But the text is unclear and perhaps the ambiguity is intentional.

43. Siva, the dancing god who dances the totality of the universe. The pacifier (*Sankara*) is one of his names: he gives peace by consciousness or death. I prefix savors by the word "essential" to recall that these are ideas, intuitively perceived, of states of being. The moods form the affective part of the dance, and the rhythmic gestures are the body of the dance. Thus Siva dances the "triple world."

44. See note 9. The two preceding stanzas could also be considered as a sequel to the response of Bharata; then it would be necessary to read in stanza 43 "I saw" instead of "I see."

45. Brahma, hearth of universal energy, even when he does not teach but reveals; he does not invest but transmits; in him essence is existence. The feminine forms which he raises to the surface of the ideal waters are the mother ideals of theatrical wisdom. They are *apsaras* ("who propel themselves on the water"). Their names follow.

46.-48. These names are known in other contexts in Hindu mythology. For example, *Ahalya* (Nonarable) is a wife of Gautama whom Indra loved in the form of her husband. Mountebank is for *Magadhi*, as the inhabitants of Magadha were well-known mountebanks and minstrels.

49. "Swati" can mean "Beautiful Gait"; it is also the name of the propitious star Arcturus. Narada ("giver of men" or of male children?) is a *Rishi* musician who, during his own lifetime, was granted immortality and asked to direct the choirs of celestial musicians (*gandharvas*, originally guardians of the nectar of immortality).

50. There are six annexed sciences which are necessary in order to grasp the intelligence of the *Veda*: pronunciation, prosody, grammar, etymology, astrology and liturgy.

51. "Master of the world" = Brahma. "Hands joined" = making the "*anjali.*"

53. The "festival of the flag" is still celebrated in India. For this occasion, one sets a staff in the ground, which represents the standard or magical lance used by Indra in his defense of the *asuras*. This staff, made of bamboo or hollow rose, is called *jarjara*, "pierced"; it is divided by its knots into five segments which are painted, from top to bottom, white, blue, yellow, red, and other gaudy colors.

54. "Titans" translates, approximately, *asuras*, who are the enemies of the *devas*, as the titans are of the gods. *Asura* originally meant "breathing, living." The *asuras*, who represent the natural forces separated from the primum mobile (while the *devas*, "luminous, celestial," are the illumined and co-ordinated forces) divide themselves into two families. One is the sons of Danu (the cut, the separated), the other the sons of Diti (the end, the bound); but they are all born from the same father, Kasapa ("tortoise" or "black-teeth"), grandson of Brahma who was commanded by him to beget the celestial beings. With Aditi (the nonbound, the infinite), he had twelve sons, whose names correspond to the twelve names of the sun. One sees that the grandfather had a great deal to do with his prolific and

tumultuous lineage. Our texts use the terms: *asuras*, sons of Danu, sons of Diti, hinderers, without much care for distinction.

55. The preliminary benediction, delivered by the head of the troupe, is usually an invocation to the tutelary divinity of the theater, summoning her favor on behalf of the public and actors. It must be composed of eight metrical units or of twelve words which form one stanza. "Conforming to sacred measures" (literally, "to the *Veda*") refers to the usage of Vedic meters or to formulas which adhere to the science of incantation. (Another reading gives "produced by the gods," instead of "auspicious," "gaudy," "rich in colors.") Each divinity, each savor has its particular rhythms, prosodically expressed by the combinations of durations and articulations. These correspondences must be especially observed in the benediction which creates the mood for the public.

56. The "sons of the end" (*daityas*) signify here and in general the *asuras* (see stanza 54). The names of the moments of action are technical terms from the art of composition. The term "provocation" is used in the "fantastic" style; it denotes a violent and magical drama. "Prologue" is not in the text, but adhering to the rules of dramaturgy and to the rest of the narration, it signifies a preliminary act in which the head of the troupe speaks to the public and to the principal dramatis personae, thereby giving the audience a complicity in the action that will follow.

58. On the standard of Indra, see stanza 53. The ewer of Brahma is also the emblem of mendicant ascetics. The "enveloping one" translates (but also limits) Varuna, the divinity of celestial waters (and secondarily, earthly ones).

59. It would be a betrayal to translate Siva ("happy, propitious") and Vishnu ("penetrating"), but Kuvera is really the "deformed prince" of the caves, guardian of hidden treasures. "Magical vehicle" is only one meaning of the word *siddhi*, which signifies, as well, with several special adaptations in the dramatic language: reach, result, magic, power to touch at a distance, magical shoe, supreme goal, etc. It is also a name for Siva. The "throne" adorned with lions or made from a lionskin is a royal seat. "River word" paraphrases Saraswati ("flowing, rich in waves") who is the wife of Brahma, the goddess of the word and the celestial river.

60. On these mythological names, see note 10.

61. These are technical terms. The dialects are the Prakrit languages spoken by minor figures and women. Only divine men, sacerdotal or royal

and, at times, female ascetics speak Sanskrit. The dramatic Prakrits (there are a dozen of them, and each play usually employs from two to four) are derived from Sanskrit by a kind of phonetic and grammatical algebra. Through skillful deformations, a series of dialects, less and less pure, are constructed; they correspond to the hierarchy of personages, from the Sauraseni of the princesses to the "language" of the vampires. These deduced dialects correspond very nearly to actual languages, a typical example of a representation of real life, obtained not by empiric imitation but by very rigorous principles of deduction. "Emotions" and "savors" are respectively *bhava* and *rasa* (see the introduction). "Form" (*rupa*) can signify "beauty" or (for *rupaka*) the diversity of dramatic genres. The three last terms are unclear; the text often plays with an ambiguity between the usual meaning of the words and the specific, technical usages.

62-63. (See stanzas 54 and 56). The hinderers (*vighnas*) are a class of *asuras*. In the Vedic hymn, the maleficent powers are represented as the "obstructors," the "hinderers," the "prisoners" of sacred action, ritual libation, and thought.

64. For "actor" one could say "dancer"; the extended meaning of the word, for dance remains at the foundation of the actor's craft. Paralyzing magic is one of the favorite weapons of alienated instincts and infernal inertia.

65. "The thread-bearer" (*sutradhara*) designates the head of the troupe (here Bharata himself). The word signifies, first of all, "architect" (who held the string of measurement): the "manager" is, in fact, an architect and a director at the same time; furthermore he "holds the strings" of the drama like the puppeteer, who has the same title, holds or manipulates the strings of his puppets. *Sutra* (cord) also designates a mnemonic text serving the "main line" of a science or craft; the head of the troupe is still "the thread-bearer," indicating that he possesses the *sutras* of the dramatic art. He "rooted himself in his thought" translates one of those expressions that is ordinarily translated by "he immersed himself in meditation." One sees how much this last way of speaking, with the images that it suggests of immobility and slowness, would be misplaced here, as it is, without a doubt, elsewhere. The "King of the gods" (Indra) leaps to the command post of his thought. If this is what you call meditation, fine. Again, for "*dhyana*," a term which is to "thought" what "clear" is to "light" would be necessary.

67. "Standard." See stanza 53. "On the staff": a variation is "on his body." Indra is represented as though bearing all of the magic jewels on his own body.

RASA or Knowledge of the Self

68-72. We have seen (note 53) that "pierced" designates a stalk pierced from one end to the other. Note here the Hindu custom of giving different explanations to the same word, not by an etymologic or semantic ignorance but in the practical goal of charging the word with its maximum imaginative power.

77. The "artisan of all" (Visvakarman) is the celestial architect and the blacksmith for the weapons of the gods. The canonical laws for the construction of the theater are given in a special chapter. Several types of halls are permitted. The building can be an open shed, a shelter of leaves, or a palace annex, but certain orientations and fundamental proportions must be observed.

79. The "striker" is Brahma. The word (*druhina*) is quite obscure; it can signify "persecutor, avenger" or "armed with a club or mallet." It designates, in any case, the redoubtable aspect of Brahma.

82. The "star of the months" (literally, "luminous mutation or measure") is the star of the moon god. The "guardians of the cardinal points" are Indra, Varuna, Kuvera, and Yama, or their respective sons placed in the east, the west, the north, and the south.

83-84. "Friend" (*Mitra*) is a name of the sun and "messenger" (*Vahni*) a name for fire, carrier of the offering and orifice of the gods. The "backstage" is the wings, green room, and dressing room. It is separated from the stage by a curtain. The "orchestra" is, in general, in front of this curtain. The "sons of the infinite" (see note 54) are the sons of Kasapa. The "howlers" (*rudras*) are the winds and storms.

86-87. "Terminator" (*Kritanta*) is the name of Yama ("the Justiciary"); "Destroyer, time" (*Kala*) a name for Mritya ("death"). "Destiny" translates *nivati*.

91. The "bounding" (*Skanda*) is the god of war, son of Siva, the pacifier. See note 43.

92. Sesha ("the other, the surviving"), Vasuki, and Takshaka ("the carpenter") are the three chiefs of the Nagas.

95. "River word": see note 59. The "ravisher" (*Hara*) is Siva. The sound *aum* unifying in one syllable the sounds *a, u, m* (earth, atmosphere, and sky; or Vishnu, Siva, and Brahma) embraces the entire *Veda* and all of the gods. The buffoon has thus a central role in the theater. He is from the Brahmanic caste, the confidant and the guide of the heroes, but his char-

acter is veiled in the grotesque and the stupid. According to Bharata, he is hunchbacked, one-eyed, and toothless; he attracts sarcasm and attack by his own clumsiness and naïveté. Possibly, the buffoon became, in the literary theater, a caricature of the court Brahmans. But, the fact that the sound *aum* is his tutelary deity suggests that his origin is totally different from that of intentional social satire. If the buffoon must play a Brahman, then, most likely, the actor originally given this role must have been a Brahman and perhaps the wisest of the troupe. Arts and religion degenerated when the humorous element (e.g., festival of fools in Catholicism) disappeared.

96. The "eminent being" is Brahma.

97-98. Traditional precept of political conduct (see *Laws of Manu*, VII, 10-109 and 198). "Rod" is for armed force in general.

104. "Good" and "Evil," (literally, "clear and not clear") characterize the natural forces rejoined to their principle (the *devas*) or separated from it (the *asuras*). The theater illustrates the doctrine of *Mimamsa,* according to which an individual, by his own actions, creates himself.

105. "Triple world": the nature of three levels, earth, atmosphere, and sky; or the society of three levels, peasant, warrior, and priest; or the man of three levels, stomach and legs, chest and arms, and head and mind.

107. "Law" translates *dharma*, which has all the meanings of the English word: natural, social, and moral law, as well as the law of the developed individual.

110. "Manifestations" (*bhava*): see the introduction. "Phases of action" has a particular technical meaning designating the stages of dramatic action.

116. The "Seven Continents" are the seven divisions of the world described in the *Puranas* (see note 10).

122. "Luminous worship," that is to say based on the principles, in contrast to the black worship of empirical magicians.

123. "Beast": literally, "wrongly directed" (which does not go in the vertical position). The symbolism of metempsychosis is taken in its literary sense only by those who are ignorant.

126. The "Solar Way" (*svarga*): the celestial world.

ORIENTAL BOOK REVIEWS

*The Tibetan Book of the Dead**

Mistrust like the plague religious and philosophical works from the Orient, except when you read them in the original text. Otherwise you choose between the translation of a learned linguist, who transforms everything into platitudes, or someone, smelling of the theosophist, who knows everything through the revelation of the divining rod, and you end up with a batter of bad English or French, Pali words in Sanskrit terminations, or Tibetan words in the metaphysical sauce of the Adyar Intelligence Service.

Fortunately, we finally have some documents from Tibet in which, with some reservations, we can have confidence: the excellent reports of Madame A. David-Neel, the translation by C. Toussaint of the *Edicts of Padma*, and, finally, the *Bardo-Thodol* ("the liberation by the understanding in the between two") or *The Tibetan Book of the Dead*, translated into English by Lama Kazi Samdup and Dr. W. Y. Evans-Wentz.

The Tibetan book is a ritual text read to the dying man or to his effigy from the first symptoms of death to the forty-ninth day after death. Its role and sometimes even its form are analogous to those of the *Egyptian Book of the Dead*. In its ritual usage the aim of the *Bardo-Thodol* is to guide a man in the decisive experience of death, to remind him of the Lamaist teaching, and to help him to profit from this unique opportunity to awaken and to escape from the cycle of rebirth. Restricted to its ritual meaning, the text reveals the scientific spirit and mathematical precision characteristic of all treatises of Oriental psychology, so different from the metaphysical reveries and empiric agnosticism of our own.

Sentimentality swept aside, physical death for the Tibetan is the

---

*First published in *Les Cahiers du Sud*, 1934. Later reprinted in *Les Pouvoirs de la parole*, Paris, Éditions Gallimard, 1972.

supreme opportunity given to all men to awaken and to understand (in Sanskrit *budh*, from which *buddha*). In the Occident morphine is given to the dying man, but in Tibet one is urged to sever the blood vessels of his neck to force the blood to flow upward to the brain, to retain his conscious state for as long as possible, to shout disagreeable and instructive things into his ears and enable him to profit from this final experience. (Where, then, the true culture, here or there? Who is the barbarian?)

The recitation of the *Thodol* to the deceased lasts forty-nine days and, the moment of death terminated, would seem to be a purely symbolic rite. But remember that this kind of text always carries a multiplicity of meanings and usages. The title says: *Bardo*, which literally means "between two" and not "death." Perhaps physical death is only the limited form of an experience, which is completely different from the "death" implied by the sages of Asia, the Old Testament, and Christianity. I say "perhaps," but the *Bardo-Thodol* would be inexplicable without this interpretation, which no one has the right or power to develop literally. I am convinced that in addition to its ritual usage, the *Bardo-Thodol* was for those who were aware of it a memento mori related to moments of human life other than physical death.

The entire work is based on the doctrine of *karma*. This word, exploited by all Occidental scholars of Buddhism, including Dr. Evans-Wentz, preserves in its Sanskrit form a perfume of philosophical exoticism and a subtle occultism which can completely ravish us and permit us to forget its meaning. I therefore remind you that the word *karma* signifies action, act, or if you will excuse these barbarisms—actioning, acting. Philologically it is equivalent (root and suffix) to the Latin *crimen* (crime, allied to crisis, critic), which signifies action through which an individual permits himself to be judged, incriminating action, *crime* but without the pejorative meaning attached today to this word. Now that you are, I hope, aware of its principal roots, perhaps you will begin to use this word without making it into one which conceals reality.

It is thus a question of an "intermediary" state through which a man becomes aware that he creates himself. How this occurs, through physical death or otherwise, is not important. Those who have tasted only a millionth part of this consciousness will understand the fundamental, terrible, and true meaning of the *Book of the Dead*. For others it is without any interest and its reading is a waste of time. The *Bardo-Thodol* gives the entire sequence of events which can in the course of a man's life give him the opportunities to awaken. The great drama is that these moments are rarely recognized. When something of absolute importance is revealed to us, just in that instant, we close our eyes, we sleep. And thus the Apostles slept when Christ on the Mount of Olives was in the fulgurant presence of his own solitude.

According to the *Bardo-Thodol*, the first revelation is the most simple and pure: being (not the being of the philosophers). Indisputable. Generally, man, because of that which he *makes himself* (*karma*), sleeps. After the "clear primordial light" comes the "secondary light." Perhaps, if one wanted to presume to understand, one would no longer call it *being* but being *a being*, in order to indicate that one no longer speaks of the absolute simplicity. Man, in general, still sleeps. This is the experience of "the moment of death" or "first bardo." The man who cannot profit from it will then experience the "second bardo" or "experience of reality." He sees himself as if in a mirror. Here the text gives a complete description of man's psychic structure: his thoughts, feelings, and physical sensation; he sees that he is made by his own mind, through his own agitated or calm or controlled responses, through the exercise of his perceptual and responsive sensibilities. If he recognizes himself, he is liberated. But most often he does not recognize himself and believes he is seeing and hearing "divinities" (those of the Lamaist pantheon, if he is a believing Tibetan), that is to say, exterior phenomena. (Remarkably, in Asiatic languages the words that mean "divinities" and "exterior apparitions" are often identical; the Sanskrit *deva*, for example, signifies "luminous" or rather "which appears"—to the human perception; and the *Upanishads* often contrast "he who looks at himself" and "he who looks at the *devas*.") Having "missed" through his own lack of consciousness these opportunities to awaken, man enters the "third bardo," that of the "search for rebirth," where diverse, less and less beautiful opportunities to become an imperfect human being are offered to him. Finally, almost always, after this "confrontation," this "being put in the presence of reality," man, shadow man, who did not know how to awaken, becomes, again as before, an idiot: sometimes a little better, but often worse; because he could become a wolf, a pig, a worm (that is to say, a man with the essence of a wolf, etc., as the naïve belief in metempsychosis is explicitly dismissed by this text, as by all intelligent Hindus and Buddhists); he can become a *preta*—a word which is generally translated by "phantom"—but which simply means left, gone: a man absent from himself, one of those larvae that pullulate around us; those who in the *Egyptian Book of the Dead* revile the "mummy" in these terms: "Faces of night, specter in the shadow, anger of anger, O maleficent doubles, who, behind me, enter in obscurity, stealthily, nose behind, face observe; O you, evil, sons of evil, generation of evil, forever deprived by that for which you arise from the depth of your night and your wickedness. O you, all, male and female, faces reversed, to whom I permit nothing, to whom I allow nothing, whom I will not allow to make night in my heart ... No, I defy you, O defeated revulsive faces ..." (translation J. C. Mardrus).

In this brief résumé we see, without having to specify it, that these opportunities to understand arise from the reality of this or that physical circumstance. Yet, everyone knows that one can say "I die" or "I am reborn to life" without necessarily implying by these words the transformation of a living body into a corpse or inversely. We also know that the sacred texts (I do not want today to define this word) are comprehended in proportion to the listener's level of being. "The bride is known only to the bridegroom at the threshold," that is to say, the sacred is understood in proportion to each man's intelligence, as the *Zohar* says. And it is always the most simple, the most direct meaning which is the most true. It is certainly true that the *Bardo-Thodol* is used in Tibet as a funerary ritual and that the term *bardo* or "between two" is popularly interpreted as designating the state after death. But if you read it in the light (feeble though it may be) of what I have tried to suggest (it is up to you), you may see that it is a question of something much more important. "Death" is the limited form of the experience, offered to each man (and woman) in each instant of "the confrontation with reality." It is true that in each instant a reality offers itself to us, but we sleep, like brutes, like the Apostles, and this opportunity is lost forever! Suddenly time itself gives us another opportunity to understand: but we close our eyes to it. And after millions and millions of instants, which are the doors of consciousness, *open for us*, but which we have not even noticed, we are still as blind as before. The last opportunity, the last instant! Will we also let it escape? The *Bardo-Thodol* poses this question. It cries out to man: remember yourself!

But it is not an abstract warning, without basis. The text gives a tableau of man in his diverse aspects and diverse modes of existence, his faculties, the form of his nonbeing, and the functioning of that machine—even a trace of which could not be found in any of our psychology. There is a knowledge of man, of secular tradition, that hardly interests the Occidental, for it is superior, practical; it demands to be lived, while our science is a research of a lesser effort. At first glance, of course, the language of this type of text, replete with words that the translators obstinately leave in Sanskrit (a language as familiar to learned Tibetans as was Latin in Europe a few centuries ago) has quite a theological air. It would suffice to translate these words literally, so that the logic and the direct, human meaning of the whole would appear (Buddha would be, simply "the awakened one," and so on). But with its lack of dedication, Occidental thought also has a hatred of simplicity.

The introduction of Dr. Evans-Wentz gives us some useful instruction on Tibetan funerary customs, their analogies with those of ancient Egypt, the history of Lamaism and its fundamental doctrines. But the author also wanted to give his interpretation of the book; and, unfortunately, he does not escape from the philosophic and occult images through which, in general, the Occidental tries to understand the Oriental doctrines. For him, there is an exoteric meaning in the *Bardo-Thodol* (which involves an interpretation so irrelevant that no one would think of supporting it, as if when I told you, "This is a bear," you were to think that "This was a plantigrade mountaineer and honey amateur") and an esoteric meaning which is an allegorical interpretation. In other words, if he pierces the theological coating external to the doctrine, he stops at the second envelope, still quite exterior: the philosophical envelope. This suffices, nevertheless, for him to make comparisons which, in many respects, assert themselves between the Tibetan and other texts—Egyptian, Socratic, or Christian. But he does not suspect the simple, human meaning, the central meaning. For when someone uses the word "esoterism" and does not hesitate to imprint black on white, and claims this to be an "esoteric interpretation," there is such a contradiction in the usage of this word that the logic and comprehension of the author become, at least for me, suspect. But all that is history or doctrinal in the introduction is very valuable, with reservations regarding the use of Sanskrit and Tibetan words, which remain untranslated in the text.

The English edition contains an introduction by Sir John Woodroffe, in the style of the purest theosophic sacristy. Nothing against it: those gentlemen know everything. They know the Sanskrit names (or Pali, one is not very sure) of the *nadis* and *chakras* and the number of lotus petals at the base of the spine; that it is dangerous for anyone, except themselves, to excite the machine because the etheric Maitreya and the ectoplasmic guru have revealed to them that they must first breathe twice through the right nostril, say: "hink," exhale by the pineal gland, putting a finger in the mouth—pardon to those of you who are offended—eat lettuce and guard against violent matters. Sweet sirs, but filthy poisoners. We must be grateful to the French translator for giving only an abridgment of this introduction and for putting it at the end of the book. We must be grateful to her, above all, for having given us this fruit of wisdom that some few still know how to find under the sterile, philosophic skins surrounding it. She did it with respect, without displaying herself, proof of an intelligence greater than any commentary.

—1934

René Daumal

*The Life of Marpa, "The Translator"**

At times the proverb, "When you offer an aperitif, you'll be reproached for not having offered a dinner," occurs to me. At times, too, I remember the vigils, labor, and patience required for a respectful translation into our vulgar languages of texts inscribed for the transmission of teachings which in the West have been, for centuries deprived of a public language. I remember—otherwise I would have ungratefully complained that this *Life of Marpa* is too fragmented. For although the extracts are connected by résumés, it often seems as if the translation stops just at the parts we were waiting to hear. We wanted to know all that could be known about Marpa, Milarepa's master, crude, learned, capable of youthful drinking bouts, awakened, indefatigable. A man who, in a Tibet swarming with religious doctrines of old and new schools, sowed the teaching, acquired with difficulty from his Indian masters: the direct method to arrive at definitive awakening in this life. But these complaints could not even be made if M. J. Bacot had not given us a few years ago a *Milarepa* translated in its entirety (at least in relation to biography), a work which is all words well weighed, a kind of gospel. The publication of *The Life of Marpa* incited me to reread *Milarepa*, and if I compare that book to a gospel, it is because it is one of those precious texts which are a measure, each time it is reread, of what has been understood more deeply in the intervening period.

I now assume that you have read (or reread) *Milarepa*. If so, these extracts from *The Life of Marpa*, which by themselves may have left you unsatisfied, will very usefully answer certain questions raised by *Milarepa*. They erase, for example, any doubts which may have been retained by some readers as to the real goodness of Marpa. The long and terrible tests which he imposed on Milarepa, his brutal behavior and appearance, sometimes resembling falsity, were not traits of his character but part of a deliberate method of instruc-

*First published in *Hermes*, II, October 1938. Later reprinted in *Les Pouvoirs de la parole*, Paris, Éditions Gallimard, 1972.

tion; a method which he applied only to Milarepa in this guise and only for a certain period of time—the time that annihilated the sorcerer, the vindictive, and the criminal Milarepa. The greatness of Marpa, like other men of sacred legend, is revealed by the way in which his humor, his character, his personality are effaced by the power of his works, his role, his realization. If we are reminded that he knew how to enjoy banquets, beer, and women, it is to tell us that he knew how to enjoy them and that he was free of them. We can only try to imagine the sufferings and labor of this man, the first Tibetan of the lineage, who made perilous voyages to India to gather for the use of his future disciples the teachings of the direct method; this old man, returning one last time to India on a longer peregrination in search of his master Naropa, who had died, finding him and obtaining, after all, the last teachings; and finally, this father, confronting his certainty, and singing his certainty; of the vanity of what the world calls world, with the body of his only son in his arms, the skull broken in eight pieces. The story tells us simply this, he did it.

Following his masters, Marpa attached great importance to the "transference of consciousness," and he taught this secret to his son; it is a question of the ability attributed to a man who has acquired at least one of the three subtle bodies (*trikaya*) which characterize a Buddha to leave his gross body and to enter into and animate an animal or human carcass. Why this importance, and what is the exact meaning of the process? I do not know. But I do know that I cannot, in my present state, know it. I also know that, for the same reason, neither Occidental science nor philosophy will ever know it. Nevertheless, it is not at all irrelevant that M. J. Bacot has translated everything in the text related to this subject and that he has added in the appendix a legend which recounts the same theme, that of a bodhisattva who has taken on the body of a cuckoo and preaches in that guise the great law to the nation of birds.

However, what I can understand, only with difficulty, is the interest that can be shown in similar texts, the troubles taken to publish and translate them by learned men who confess their rejection of the teachings transmitted by these texts and see in them only manifestations of a "mentality" different from our "own," from "ours" (they do not say only from "theirs"). In their eyes, with their refined logic, a Milarepa would have to be a madman, a fool, an ecstatic, and the doctrine described in these narratives absurd fantasies unworthy of serious study. Why this curiosity and this mania for collecting in the Occidental philosophers? Is this their literary sensibility? Others, for whom the texts are relevant, profit from their work; but these others are a bit saddened to have had to say to M. J. Bacot and to the best of his colleagues: *Sic vos, non vobis, mellificatis*… Because, if these scholars admitted the truth of the doctrines and the stories in which they are interested, they would not rest until they had found the teachings capable of helping them to be liberated from the enslavement, the unconsciousness, the inconsistency, and the incoherence of *samsara*—of our life (and here we agree to say "our" and not only "their"). I would say the same to those men of letters, among whom Milarepa and the Tibetan ascetics have been in fashion these last years, who found poetic beauty and sources of great feeling in them but were not troubled by there being something else: *the truth*. Today, the "interesting" and the "curious" outshine the true; the "strange" and the "shocking" shadow the true. We are interested in doctrines which we do not adopt; we admire examples that we do not follow. In fact, in our time, nothing is valued more than the truth. Without a doubt, truth sells.

—1938

Buddhism, Its Doctrines and Methods*

This would only be another book on Buddhism if the author had not been a Buddhist, had not lived a great part of her life in Buddhist countries, and had not already published four or five animated books which this one completes and illumines on her life in Tibet.

Thinking and living as a Buddhist does not deny a deep sense of Occidental culture and a very developed critical spirit. Mrs. David-Neel approaches Buddhism as a method, an art of living: true of all doctrines useful for deliverance—the rest is error or lost time. The Buddha said it in similar terms. Our century needs this shouted in its ears. It would be desirable to shout, loudly, another Buddhist rule: be your own lamp and *disbelieve* everything that you have not actually experienced; for our "science" applies this rule exclusively to a knowledge of external objects.

The Buddhist doctrines, with their common base and their divergences, are elucidated by principles of superior utility and direct experience. Mrs. David-Neel shows this essential very clearly with a marked and justified preference for the oral doctrines of the "Great Vehicle," which gives adaptations of the Buddhist teaching to the social and religious traditions of the northern Buddhist countries.

After reading the book, and reflecting on its contents, I realized that these great principles have nothing which is especially Buddhist; it is only our civilization which ignores them. Buddhism adopted them from the Hindu tradition, from which it later separated. Why don't we, then, take them from the Brahmanic sources, instead of searching for them in the Buddhist heresy? The Hindu tradition, because it is tradition, embodies all aspects of life, and in particular the stages, professions, ceremonies, and institutions. The result is that the Brahmanical texts, with their purely Indian references, are not very accessible to the Occidental. Whereas Buddhism, in

---

*First published in *La Nouvelle Revue Française*, 1936. Later reprinted in *Les Pouvoirs de la parole*, Paris, Éditions Gallimard, 1972.

separating itself from the social life of India, established a more universal expression; in appearance at least, for it will become truly universal only when it integrates itself into the quotidian life of the individual and his society: the Buddhist heresy becomes then a tradition culture, as in Tibet, in the form of Lamaism. Heresy is the messenger of tradition: where it settles, it dies in fertilizing the seed of a new tradition.

It is necessary—and this is simply to take Buddhism to the letter—to judge the Buddhist teaching by its actual utility. If not, certain of their formulas will be in great danger. Thus the disdain of Buddhism (that of the South, at least) for social life; and its mistrust (theoretically) of the old Hindu rule of the human stages, according to which a man could not "retire into the forest until having experienced a normal human life" and having seen "the children of his children"; and too, the formula of the "nonreality of the I," which has led unhappy theosophists to moral and spiritual annihilation. A formula, so well corrected by this definition of *nirvana*, cited by Mrs. David-Neel: "*Nirvana* means the perception of reality as it truly *is*. And when, by a complete change (a turning inside-out) in all methods of mental process, there follows an understanding of oneself (by oneself)—this I call *nirvana*."

A philosopher might regret that the speculative doctrines of Buddhism, with its various cosmological and theological schools, have not been explicated by the author. But this is of little importance, as it has been done in many other works. Mrs. David-Neel, with good reason, wished to speak to us about Buddhist life and not about Buddhist "philosophy" (which thrives especially well in our European imagination).

In the appendix, the author gives numerous citations, translations from Pali, Sanskrit, Chinese, and Tibetan; and several pages—one would have liked more—on the Zen sect. A patriarch of this sect said:

"To look for illumination by separating oneself from this world is as absurd as to search for the horns of a hare." And: "Do not think of good, do not think of evil, but look, in the present moment, at your original face—the one you had before you were born."

For this last citation alone, the book is a treasure, a treasure difficult to find.

—1936

RASA or Knowledge of the Self

Two Tibetan Texts

on

the Conversion of the Birds*

M.J. Bacot gives, in the appendix to *The Life of Marpa*, the text and translation of a Tibetan text, *The Avadana of the Bird Nilakantha*. In this tale the prince of Benares (an incarnation of the bodhisattva Avalokiteshvara) loses his human body through the betrayal of an ambitious official and is obliged to adopt, instead, the body of a cuckoo bird which he had earlier, only in play, assumed. Permutations of the corporeal envelope are frequent in Tibetan legends; but, as they are attributed to men who have arrived at a level of reality superior to our own, we cannot really discuss them nor know if the learned lamas take them as literal or symbolic facts. How then shall we interpret such a narrative? As a literary artifice? Or, to the letter, as the expression of a naïve belief? I read them first one way, then the other; that is to say, first, as a learned work, and then as a popular legend which serves as a vehicle for the teaching. Then—and I should have begun in this way, but one does not become simple in an instant—I remembered that this type of text was written in the universal language of symbols, and I began to see clearly. If a great part of this story remains obscure to me, it is due to the imperfection of my reasoning and not to lack of documentation or interpretive ingenuity. The actual facts of the narration are apparent: there are two men, seemingly friends. One is the son of the king, the other wants to supersede him. This rival is the son of the first tutor of the palace. He is pressured by an ambitious, foreign princess. The rival is more malicious than the prince, who is still credulous and inexperienced. They go to visit an unexplored forest of the royal domain. They must be back before evening. They cross a river. They leave their bodies on the bank and in the form of two birds, they cross the river. The treacherous minister steals the body of the

---

*First published in *La Nouvelle Revue Française*, 1936. Later reprinted in *Les Pouvoirs de la parole*, Paris, Éditions Gallimard, 1972.

prince in order to reign in his place. The other body is cast into the river. The prince remains a bird among birds. All this had been predicted. In all languages, the significant words "two men," "son of the king," "a river," "two birds," etc. are, at the same time, words from a universal *language*, of which the principal characteristic is that the name cannot be understood without the thing.

The teaching by the prince become cuckoo of the true law is the subject of *The Precious Garland of the Law of the Birds*, of which Henriette Meyers has made the first European translation. It is truly a Tibetan poem, and not, like many of the Lamaist texts, an adaptation of one that was originally Indian. It is also a true poem and not a simple allegory. There is in the presentation of those great assemblies of birds an enchantment that the translator was able to preserve for us (despite great difficulties) and through which the listener or the reader is put in a state which is propitious for the reception of the doctrine. The teaching is moral and practical, evidently designed for a large public. The assembled birds repeat, in turn, to their master the principles which they have understood—each one choosing a brief motif which he develops in a few verses. "It is necessary to understand (this, this, this)," "(This) without (that), what misery!" "Because one seeks (this), one finds (that)," etc. Thus each bird summarizes in his way an essential aspect of the doctrine. The great bird illumines these partial insights by this first Buddhist law: admit illusion, see that we live in dream. The following year he takes the same theme and gives it a positive conclusion (that we too often forget when we speak of Buddhism): the urgency to "realize one's own being" while this body is alive, and the absolute necessity to resort to the three real refuges: the Buddha, the true law, and the community of those who search. Then the birds take vows which summarize for each one his particular teaching, singing and dancing before the great bird, their teacher, before dispersing.

This beautiful poem, while destined to recollect certain rules of life, is never "the moralizer." That is to say, behind the injunction there is always the principle. Likewise, within a facile literary form, an apparent fantasy, there is always the doctrine which the author does not obscure. We must remember that for the differing degrees of doctrinal understanding there are two orders of exposition: a logical order which descends from absolute reality to the illusion where we live, passing through degrees of relative sensibility (this is the order followed by the Hindus in their metaphysical treatises); and a methodical order of teaching and work which necessarily begins with our actual state. According to this second order, Buddhism successively affirms: "There are only relative realities: to be awakened is to be awakened in relation to a dream;"[1] there is an absolute reality: to be awakened (*buddha*) is to be awakened absolutely, it is to possess the *dharmakaya*, the universal body, the "uniquely indestructible." Buddhism was heretical because it stopped at the first or second of these degrees of understanding; it is this Buddhism which was driven from India and which has had such success in the West. Buddhism, in the form of "The Great Vehicle" (to which Lamaism is related), by reasserting the universality, no longer contains anything which opposes it to other forms of the universal doctrine; most of the apparent contradictions are explained by these few remarks.

—1938

René Daumal

NOTE

[1] Do you ask for precisions? It is not the best moment to speak of symbolic language, as the text in question is not firsthand, nor is it a purely symbolic text, without a mixture of "literature." Further, I do not presume to know any more than the rudiments of this language. One cannot set up a dictionary of symbols; this would be to reduce them to metaphor or to allegory. The definition of a word is made according to the process of logical formulae: by reference to classes and by the attribution of its components. The definition of a symbol is made according to the laws of analogy. These two orders of meaning are different. The definitions of words and symbols become meaningful and reunite when the signified thing is present; as in geometry, the word "triangle" and a triangular figure, when the idea of the triangle is real. In the present context, the signified thing can only be actualized through the experience of each reader. All that I can do is to refer each symbol to other cases of its expression. Thus, only as an example and using very accessible texts: "the two men": *New Testament, passim* (Ephesians 4: 20-24; Colossians 3: 9-11, etc.); "the foreign woman . . . who speaks in a sweet and flattering language": Proverbs 8; "the river to cross": Psalms 123: 4-7 (with a reference, as well, to "the bird"; *Svetasvatara Upanishad*, I, 5; II, 8); "the son of the king": *Zohar*, II, 163, and II, 185 (I chose these two passages as they also speak of a titled temptress); "the bird": this is a symbol which, frankly, I don't understand and which the Kabbala says is "above human understanding" (the bird and the Messiah, *Zohar,* II, 8-9, etc.); "the two birds": *Mundaka Upanishad*, III, I, 1-2; *Svetasvatara Upanishad*, IV, 6-7.

RASA or Knowledge of the Self

Hymns and Prayer of the Veda*

Confronted with the Vedic hymns, ordinary thought—including that of our greatest "thinkers"—must abdicate. These are poems like old Babylonian, Hebrew, or Chinese poems, and men such as we cannot create, and therefore cannot comprehend, a true poem. Their origin, say the Hindus, is "nonhuman" (*apurusheya*).

We must approach these hymns in the available texts and with the insufficient aid of Vedic philology. We must open ourselves before these words whose drone can completely penetrate the heart, shattering our fragile logic on its way. We must, poor Sherlock Holmes, admit defeat before these mysteries, fully and finally to appreciate the humility of Louis Renou's translation. We must pay homage to him, having blushed at the impudence with which so many others have wanted "to explain" these Vedic hymns, as if they were astronomers who, in order to examine the sun, tried to illumine it with candles.

It seems to me that Louis Renou has chosen for each word and for each syntactic form, from the myriad possibilities, the words and forms that are the least probable in the present context of Vedic exegesis. His predecessors based their translations on false, partial ideas. He does not base his on any preconceived (false or true) theory; and this certainly will give the public a less distorted (and a more true) image of Vedic poetry. Not to know is an illness, an illness we all share; to pretend to know is a crime. We accept with good grace this last resort, as it is unlikely that there will be for a long time a man able to understand the thought of the *Vedas* (and this would not be a man in the ordinary sense of the word) who knows the Vedic and French languages well enough to give us a perfect translation.

The hymns are well chosen; they are a presentation of the varieties in tone and the real aim of the thousands of poems which

---

*First published in *La Nouvelle Revue Française*, 1936. Later reprinted in *Les Pouvoirs de la parole*, Paris, Éditions Gallimard, 1972.

are collected in the four volumes of the *Vedas*. What remains to be done, in order more deeply to penetrate Vedic thought, are translations which would no longer be horizontal but vertical. Instead of translating one hymn after the other, translate a hymn, then its more authoritative commentaries (like those of Sayana), then the passages of the *Brahmana* and the *Upanishads* related to this hymn, with their glossaries and the commentaries on these glossaries; and finally, the principal psychological, mythological, and juridical texts, building on the authority of the original word. Such a work would give an idea of what for an orthodox Hindu is implied by the authority of the *Vedas*.

—1939

THE HYMN OF MAN*
A *"Vertical"* Translation

INTRODUCTION

The following sections are studies of Daumal's Sanskrit translations from the Rig Veda, the Upanishads, the Sahitya-darpana, etc. The translation of these texts, and in particular of the Sanskrit commentaries which Daumal also translated, presented rather unique problems. The translator has tried to make these texts accessible to the English reader having no knowledge of Sanskrit, not to mention the Sanskrit student or scholar who may have a thorough knowledge of these texts, both in their original language and in other existing English versions of the hymns or poems.

These works were not published during Daumal's lifetime. They were edited by Jacques Masui and collected in a volume entitled Bharata (Paris: Éditions Gallimard, 1970). The English versions were based upon that edition and on Daumal's personal manuscripts for the works. Oddities of punctuation etc. have sometimes been retained for the sake of authenticity, as it is impossible to know how Daumal would have resolved the various surface details of his personal work.

The form of the following texts may seem, at first glance, somewhat confusing to the reader. It actually illustrates a method with which Daumal was working in order to translate Sanskrit in a way which would retain its organic power—"the power of the word" (see his preface to "To the Liquid" and the essay on A. Renou, "Hymns and Prayer of the Veda").

The typographical layout of the French posthumous publication, the model for this one, tried to reflect the form with which Daumal chose to translate "The Hymn of Man." The punctuation for the Sridhara and Sayana commentaries follow those of the French edition, which was based on Daumal's personal manuscript for the work.

"The Hymn of Man," generally called the Purusa Sukta, is the nineteenth hymn of the tenth mandala of the Rig Veda.

—LLL

---

*First published in *Bharata*, Paris, Éditions Gallimard, 1970.

RASA or Knowledge of the Self

NOTES FOR THE READING OF
THIS TRANSLATION

1. The words placed beneath a word of the text denote principal images or thoughts evoked by the word, in addition to its principal meaning—by associations of meaning, sound, or etymology.

2. The words in quotation marks denote a literal or strictly etymological translation (the meaning of which may be "forgotten" by a Hindu reader but which still asserts itself, invisibly, in the texture of the word). Example: *bhumi*: the earth, the "existing" (Latin: *humus*, from which *homo*, man, *humanus*, *humilis*), from the root *bhu*, to exist (in time and space), to become, to extend, from which *bhuman*: greatness, riches, fertility, immensity—from which *bhuta*: element (material: earth, water, fire, air, ether), etc.

3. The words in parentheses are not in the text but are implied (usually for simple grammatical reasons).

4. The words united by dashes translate a single Sanskrit term. One finds in Sanskrit, especially in the "classical era," words which would have to be translated into English by "In-the-middle-of-a-wood-which-accords-well-being-through-the-ensemble-of-chattering-cuckoos-joined-with-the-humming-produced-by-swarms-of-bees-intoxicated-with-honey."

5. Asterisks beneath certain words refer to commentaries which follow the translation.

René Daumal

Here, in the VISION-OF-THE-STANZAS (= Rig Veda)
    (knowledge)
    sacred knowledge
is the "true evocation" of man
    (well-chanted)   male principle, active
    (= hymn)   resident, fulfiller,
                  citizen occupant

1. Thousand-headed,   man,   thousand-eyed,
    (summits?)   male-active   axes
                   resident, fulfiller,   circles
                   citizen

thousand-membered,
    "feet"—parts

from-everywhere covering the earth,
        "the existing"
        the becoming

he is-higher than-the-ten-fingers (of his stature).
    *
    ten fingers = one *pradesa* = one span
    pradesa = *pra* + a*desa* (= indicator, index finger)
    (but also): *pri*mordial in*di*caction (unit of measure)
    thus: the unit of measure expressed by the decade

    "The space within the heart" is said to measure a "unity" and to be greater than all worlds.

2. Man (is) truly all-this, the once-become, the to-become,
  male-active-   the world—   past   future
  resident-fulfiller the manifestation—
  citizen   the namable—all "hoc"
                 the present

RASA or Knowledge of the Self

and also master-of-the-immortal, he whom nourishment

    possessor   *amrta* (ἄμβροτος)
    dispenser   "immortality" and
    lord   divine nectar

makes more.

"increased"

3. Such (is) his greatness, but still—more is man.

    breadth-   older,   male-
    plenitude-   more ancient,   active-
    magnitude-   more grand,   resident-
    power   more respectable,   fulfiller-
         more real   citizen

(One of his) member(s) (is) all existences,

    "Foot"—part   the beings
    QUARTER   beings-in-becoming
         (*bhuta* = φύσις)
         creatures—the living

(his) three (other) members, (are) immortal in the sky.

    "Foot"—part   *immortality*   "the shining"
    QUARTER   nectar   the luminescent
         region
         the luminous state

4. On-three-members man exalted himself,

    with   "Feet" —   "emerged directly
    gifted with   parts   for the height"
         QUARTERS

on-one-member he yet exists in-this-world

    with   still
    gifted with

René Daumal

then he progressed,   **in-every-sense, he penetrated**

    *

"advanced, separating   "by dividing himself
himself, toward…"   into diverse paths"

that-which-eats-and-that-which-does-not-eat.

    *

living beings   celestial beings, cosmic forces,
                inanimate things

5. The illuminate was born from-him, and from the illuminate

    *

the diversifier (Viraj)   id.★
the being, brahman,   ←
penetrating, manifesting and
ordering the diversity of the world

the super-man, who (no sooner) born increased,

  *   *

male-active   grew excessively
resident-   transcending himself
fulfiller
citizen

(composing) next the earth—(of existence)

(surpassing,   the existing
creating while transcending,
leaving behind)[1]

and then the cities (of men).

city = *pura* = "full"
And, man = *pu*r*u*sa (fulfiller)
thus, the "occupied" by the "citizen" (man), thus:
THE HUMAN BODIES

★[*idem*, Lat. "same person"]

[1] This is the meaning given by an Hindu commentator. The line (Stanza 5, line 2) could also mean: who (no sooner) born increased, traversing the earth from West to East. (When born, he ranges earth from East to West," says Coomaraswamy: this is not a reference. I prefer to follow the traditional commentary.)

6. When, with-man as-the-offering,

        male-active
        resident-fulfiller
        citizen

the gods	**presented**	**the sacrifice,**
deva	displayed—	act of veneration
"who shines"	spread out	sacred action
who shines for the perception in general:	prepared	

who appeared, who emitted light or force, in general. Thus: star, reality, exterior (one often contrasts "that which sees the *devas*"—exterior, "objective" and "that which sees the self"—interior, "subjective") cosmic force—an energy center in the cosmos, or in man: an organ or function of the senses—a vital function. Thus, a force or reality which is not actually conscious, but which becomes so by annihilating man's consciousness of his individuality.

spring was	**the (ritual) butter,**	**summer the combustible,**	
(the season) of "richness, fertility"	purified butter used in the sacrifice	"the heat"	the sacrificial wood which was used to ignite the fire into which the butter was poured

autumn	**the oblation.**
the "rupture" (of the rains) later: the cessation of the rains[2]	the *moment* or the act of pouring the offering of butter onto the sacrificial fire

7. This sacrifice which they spread on the rushes

veneration, sacred action	offered, poured, immolated	"the displayed" force? the carpet of sacred herbs from the Vedic altar

---

[2]This is the old subdivision of the year, which is based on the order of the monsoon. There are thus only three seasons and winter is not designated.

René Daumal

was man, born-in-the-beginning,
> male-active   "at the point"
> resident-fulfiller
> citizen

god,   **propitiators**   **and primordial-singers**
                                                                                                                                                *

devas[3]   "those whom one   (*Rishis*, initiators)
"shining,"   must make propi-   prophets—those who
cosmic   tious"   *   saw the original
forces,   (the *Sadhyas*)   sounds of the *Veda*
etc.   the Greek demons,
                 the Judeo-Christian-
                 Islamic angels

sacrificed him.

8. **From this sacrifice to-the-total-offering**
>   veneration   "in which the offered entity
>   sacred action   is the total being (universal
>   man) all that exists"

curdled-milk-and-butter took shape.
> (sacrificial substances)

It spawned the animals governed-by-wind,
                                                         *
>   Birds (flocks of birds) (*vayu*)
>   —or even cattle, whose
>   tutelary deity is the
>   wind (because clouds are celestial flocks:
>   backlash of metaphors)

and those of the forest and villages.
>   wild beasts   domestic animals

---

[3] It might be necessary to read: the propitiator gods (who are the propitiators), but it is doubtful.

RASA or Knowledge of the Self

9. From this sacrifice to-the-total-offering,
        veneration   in which the offered
        sacred action   entity is universal
                                    man

stanzas,   **melodies,**   **rhythms**
the hymns of   the liturgies   poetics: that which
the *Rig Veda*   of the *Sama Veda*   unfortunately we usually
                                            call meters

and sacrificial-words were born.
        the magical, ritual
        formulas of the
        Yajur Veda

10. Horses and those-with-two-rows-of-teeth,
            (animals having two rows of teeth)

cows, sheep-and-goats were born from it.
            (from this sacrifice—or from man)

11. When they immolated   **man,**
        dismembered,   male-active
        offered   resident-fulfiller
                            citizen

what were his components?

What were his mouth, (his) arms,
        face   "the strong"
        (origin)

(his) thighs and (his) feet named?
      "the great
      supports"?

René Daumal

12. His mouth was the priest, (his) arms became the royalty,

        the brahman   the caste of
        "the sacred speaker"   the *Kshatriyas*
                                            (rajan = rex,
                                            regis-ruler
                                            (roi) = he
                                            who angers,
                                            reddens, is
                                            enraged)

his thighs, they were the people,

    Vaisyas = (the descendants
    of those) who entered—those
    who populated the country:
    peasants or those who went
    everywhere: the merchants

from (his) feet the servile were born.

    Sudras—the ignoble caste,
    unregenerated
    servants of the other three

13. From (his) psyche   the moon was born,

passive thought, reflection,   "The-brightness-that-measures"
mental matter—which is to the
active intelligence that which
the moon is to the sun
(*manas*: cf. moon)

from (his) eyes the sun,

        (*surya* = solar, sun)
        the shining or resonant

fire and   power from (his) mouth,

Agni,   Indra—the empyrean—
the actor,   the ether—the universal
the agent,   energy: *indriya* means
the inciter   man's faculties, etc.

and from (his) breath   the wind.

    respiration   *vayu*
    (inspiration)   the "breathing"; also
    vital breath, life   designates the "animal spirits"

RASA or Knowledge of the Self

14. From (his) navel the atmosphere, from (his) skull

    hub   the "intermediary"
(between earth and
sky)—the "transparent"

the sky   took shape,

"brilliant,   (conformed,
luminous"   filled-out)

from (his) feet the earth;   directions from (his) hearing,

    the existing,   or regions of space
    the great   (four cardinal points
        plus zenith and nadir)

thus they ordered   the worlds.

the conquered   *loka* (from *lok*, cf. look) to see,
gods and   the visible—or: the peoples-places
realized

15. There were seven circular ditches, and three-times-seven

    (ditches which surrounded the
    altar—perhaps canals for blood?)

torches, when the gods,   presenting this sacrifice,

logs lit for   "shining"   offering   sacred action
the sacred fire   cosmic   spreading   act of veneration
    forces,
    centers
    of energy,
    faculties,
    etc.

bound man (as)   sacrificial beast.

active, male-   "cattle" (domestic animals and, first
resident   of all, animals used in the sacrifice):
fulfiller-citizen   the name *pasu* (Latin *pecus*) = literally:
    joined, bound (to be immolated?)

René Daumal

16. At the sacrifice, they sacrificed the sacrifice, the gods!

"shining" cosmic
forces, centers of
energy, faculties, etc.

Here were the first laws

"that which upholds"
(*dharma*) (duty, virtue)
law (natural, human, religious or individual)

and, thus exalted,   they attained the (place) "not-without-joy"

magnified –	(state) "who is not joyless":
acceding to happiness –	the place (state) of
to power (to consciousness?)	beatitude—heaven, felicity

where they, the gods, are the ancient propitiators.

"shining" cosmic forces, centers of energy, faculties, etc.	*santi:* in the strong sense of the verb "to be"	"who must be made propitious" the Greek δαίμων, Judeo-Christian, Islamic *angels*

Notes: Extracts from the Commentaries of Sridhara and Sayana

Stanza 1, Verse 2:
"he is higher..." (One could also say:"he surpasses it—the Earth—by ten fingers," but:) Having fully realized the reach of a span (a "unity of measure"), he yet exceeds it. Here the text indicates not man's measure but the fact that he "surpasses." (Sridhara)
(His essence is to be beyond—whatever it is—always to transcend his own greatness.)

Stanza 2, Verse 2:
"and also ...": "Also," that is to say, he is the possessor and the sovereign master of immortality.

"he whom ...": "He whom ..." (means): because of this he is made more; he develops by exteriorizing himself through nourishment, that is to say, through the nourishment absorbed by all living beings or through that which they (in general) enjoy.

"more": The prefix "more" (signifies): having crossed over (departed from and surpassed). This means that, having departed from the causal state, which is his own (state), he obtains the omnivision of the state of movement (of the universe). (He attains the state in which he is actually visible and as if enveloped by this appearance.) This is why he goes from the causal state to the state of movement (of the universe) so that living beings may taste the fruit of their actions; thus his essence (his reality) is the substance at the heart of all. (His substantial reality transcends the relative aspect with which he envelops himself.) (Sayana)
Ibid.: "He is not only the totality of all that exists, he is the sovereign master of immortality, that is to say, of the beatitude which is his true nature." (Sridhara)

Stanza 4, Verse 1:
"on one member": A foot (member) of his (= the fourth part of his substance); "yet exists in-this-world": which means that due to phenomena of projection (creation, emanation) and dissolution, his substance continued to return ... Then, reassuming his magical power (*maya*), he multiplied, that is, he became distinct and multiple in the forms of gods,

men, and animals, and penetrated, that is, occupied, by which action? By taking, as his goal, first, the being who lives from nourishment, the being gifted with the sensibility to which the functions of nutrition and others belong; or yet: the being gifted with (conscious) life, in other words, with knowledge."[1]

Stanza 4, Verse 2:
"in every sense": "In every sense" means he who directs himself to the basis of the differentiation (who goes completely to each distinct form). (Sridhara)

"that which eats and that which does not eat"—and secondly, "that which does not live from nourishment": That is, the being who is gifted neither with sensibility nor with (conscious) life, such as mountains, rivers and other material bodies." (Sayana)

Stanza 5, Verse 1:
"The illuminate . . . from-him": This stanza is a development of the preceding one. "The illuminate (*Viraj*) was born *from-him*," that is, from man (*purusa*), whose body is the egg of Brahma (= the "speaker"?). This being is called the illuminate (*Viraj*) because all substances appear distinctly (are illumined and diversified) in it.

Stanza 5, Verse 2:
"super-man": Man (*purusa*), establishing himself as the supreme director of this body, the "super-man" (*adi purusa*) was born as a human personality (self, individual spirit) and became the person-who-claimed-this-body. The being who in the "depth-of-knowledge" (*Vedanta*) is called the supreme self (essence), having created by its magic (*maya*) the body of the illuminate (*Viraj*), which is the egg of Brahma, and having entered it in the form of the individual self (essence, spirit, personality) became the life (*jiva*: the conscious life, i.e., the consciousness of life), the essential living spirit (living-in-and-for-itself) who claims this egg of Brahma ("speaker").

"who born": "Who (when) he (was) born," this man-illuminator (diversifier: *virat-purusa*).

"increased": (This personality, the male principle of the illuminate-diversifier) "increased" (became excessive), that is, augmented (multiplied himself), and appeared in the diverse forms of gods, men and animals.

[1]Which is a form of food.

"next": "Next," that is, having become the individual spirit (the self) of gods and other beings, he produced the earth ("the-great-existing").

"then": "Then," that is, immediately after producing the earth, he produced the cities for the (self) individual spirits.

"cities": By "cities" (*pu*ras) one implies the bodies, because they are filled (*pur*yanti) by the seven substances of which they are constituted. (Sayana)

Stanza 7, Verse 2:
"propitious": The "propitious"(*Sadhyas*) are the-lords-of-the-creation (*prajapati*) and others destined to be the instruments of the production (creation), the (demiurges).

"Primordial-singers": The "primordial-singers" (prophets, initiators, Rishis)[2] are those-who-see-the-charms (the *mantras*). (Sayana)

Stanza 8, Verse 2:
"governed by the wind": The wind (*vayu*), through the atmosphere, becomes the divinity of the flocks. This is written in the *Brahmana* (theological commentary) of the *Yajur Veda* ("knowledge of the sacrificial formulas") which states: "The wind is the sovereign of the atmosphere." And, the atmosphere is the divinity of the flocks: it is the winds which envelop them. (Sayana)

Here then is a short translation sketch, incorporating samples of traditional commentaries. I can't help feeling, however, that more often than not, these commentators want to deceive us, obscuring, with metaphysical complexity, the simplest, most direct meaning.

---

[2]Coomaraswamy translates by "prophets," which corresponds closely enough to the etymological meaning (pro-phet: he who speaks first).

TO THE LIQUID*

The two translations which follow are studies of Hymn LXIX of the IXth Mandala of the Rig Veda. They are addressed "To the Liquid" or "The Soma," the magical substance to which an entire cycle (mandala) of the Rig Veda is dedicated. Considered by some to refer to an actual plant substance, considered by others to be an organic corporeal substance or even, metaphorically, an ambrosial or ethereal substance, this potion exerted a powerful influence on the creators of the Vedic texts.

The translations were published posthumously in Bharata. They were studies of the Rig Veda, translated by Daumal at an interval of about ten years. The preface to this work was extracted by the editor of Bharata from Daumal's personal notes, in this case, an unsent letter, dated around 1942, to Jean Paulhan.

— LLL

Extract from the Rig Veda

Preface

... I said to myself that, perhaps, I would reverse my refusal to give you some translations from the Vedic hymns. Here are a few quick sketches; they are among the most difficult and obscure of the *Rig Veda* hymns (9th Mandala), probably because they are the most *simple* in essence. If I withhold them until I am fully satisfied, they will most likely never be seen; and I think that I will be able to do a little better than what, until now, has been done (thanks to the admirable work of those learned men whom I respect for their

---
*First published in *Bharata*, Paris, Éditions Gallimard, 1970.

sweet and precocious mania for erudition; but not at all for their intelligence).

I would see the publication in this form:

> I. Introduction (neither historic nor linguistic nor metaphysical but, instead, very simple) like the thought and speech of infants, or of the Vedic poets who are, in fact, infants saved by and in the adult consciousness.
>
> II. Translations of some hymns (from the same cycle for more homogeneity).
>
> III. Translation of the principal Hindu commentaries for those hymns: liturgical, metaphysical, or poetic. (A note, in this regard, on what constitutes a sacred text and on the orthodoxy of the different commentators, despite their apparent contradictions. How each interpretation corresponds to a stage of human life.)
> (These three parts would contain no word of Sanskrit.)
>
> IV. (Necessary to reassure the erudite readers) Critical analysis of one or two stanzas, and the different translations that have been proposed for them—an example, the following, a sketch for this work.

But this would require a rather lengthy work (hours for each line because it is necessary to trace each mantra throughout Hindu literature).

For these translations, there is one primary condition: to understand. All that is confused, awkward, vague, in the following, is that which I have not yet understood.

The word "god" would require an explication. I would translate it, first, etymologically by "luminous" or by "celestial (from the light)"—but (the word) "god" is the exact etymologic equivalent of *deva*; and *deva*, even in the *Veda*, signifies at times a being.

(It could be a man, a horse, a bull, as well as a star, a flame, a force, a life, etc.—i.e., all that appears or makes appear.) But the dominating image of the word is: light and, above all, light of the sky (*div*, *dyu*).

René Daumal

Hymn LXIX

Arrow? No:* it is thought* which is set against* the bow—
Calf that one delivers?* No: the thought leaps to its mother's udder;
Like a wide river it milks the tip of its course,*
The liquid in its own vows* is released.

The thought is shot, the wine is poured,
The force of the drink combusts in the mouth,
The clear wave rings with the killer's roar,
A wine drop drips on the goatskin gourd.

On the skin of the ewe, the mate-seeker, radiant,
The limitless one's daughter freed as he enters the way,
The war horse of gold has neighed, uniting sacred pourer and potion,
Sharpening the male powers, like a buffalo, he shines.

The bull bellows, the milking cows answer his call,
To the gods, adorned and attending, the goddesses come,
—the liquid traverses the ewe's brilliant skin,
Clothed, not with cloth, but with its own wave.

The war horse of gold, immortal, when leaving the wave,
Is clothed in a cloth without age and which blinds,
He made for the two cups a carpet of clouds
And, by his growth, the skies top to adorn his departure.

Like those of the sun, the rays, eager to flow,
Intoxicated, animated the soldiers of sleep,
And the fabric stretched out—rapid emissions,
Without Indra no thing becomes clear.

*The asterisks refer to commentaries which follow the translation.

RASA or Knowledge of the Self

Rapid, as in the river's descending wave,
The liquors which rose from the fecund bull found a way,
Joy in our hearts for the two and four-footed!
For us, O liquid, let the foods and harvests come up.

Brighten the treasures, the streams of gold,
Horses, cows, wheat, and the powers of procreation!
You—O you, liquid!—you, my fathers, arise!
Chiefs of the sky, arise! Makers of nourishment!

In clear waves these liquids have gone to Indra,
Like chariots in conquest, poured,
They pass through the ewe's illumined filter,
Rejecting the envelope, the war horses of gold charge the rain.

O shining, for powerful Indra, enlightened,
Giver of joy! Destroyer! With absolute words!
Bring to your singer resplendent goods,
That heaven and earth may satiate us with gods!

René Daumal

NOTES
(fragments)

"Arrow? No: it is thought." This is the phrasing which, in the Vedic syntax, is always used to introduce a metaphor: "this arrow, or rather no, I wish to say: the thought . . . ." Ordinarily, one would translate: "Like an arrow . . . similar to an arrow . . . ," but this form is used exclusively for the translations of comparisons which are actually introduced by "like," or by "the same as." On the other hand, the first word of the stanza, called "seed of the formula," has for the Hindu a determining importance on the particular development of the stanza, and, insofar as possible, it should be retained in the translations.

"against the bow" and not simply "on" the bow: "against" also implies reciprocity; the bow and arrow form a couple; the arc is the *soma*, the offering, the resuscitating nourishment given to the fire; the arrow is the hymn, whether it is (in the physical order) the sputtering voice of fire, (in the liturgical order) the chant of the officiating priest (adhering to Hindu commentaries) or (in the microcosmic order, the most real—*cf. Upanishads, Bhagavad Gita*, etc.) the thought-will emitted by man, the flame which he nourishes by interior offerings of his vital *soma*.

"Calf? No." (the same remarks that precede on the metaphor by negation). Following Sayana, it is necessary to understand: "A calf left at the udder . . . ," which is contested by Renaud, who translates: "like the calf, it was released at the udder . . . ." But the two ideas are linked to the same root "to liberate, to *let go*, to deliver"; on the other hand, if the word "udder" is in the locative this does not necessarily translate "at the udder," the presence of the preposition "near (very near) to" having been given. The metaphor is coherent; the offering—*soma*, vital force, released the thought, which immediately returned, in order to be nourished, to its mother.

"it milks the tip of its course," word for word: "it (has) milked, going at (or toward) the tip (the end)." Here also, the value of the locative is modified, perhaps by the prefix.

"in (the way of) its own vows (laws)": to the contrary, here, the locative has its full sense and cannot be translated by "according to the laws . . . " nor by "toward the laws"—still less by "for (i.e., in order to accomplish) this sacred work."

RASA or Knowledge of the Self

Rig Veda
("The Vision of the Stanzas")
9th MANDALA
HYMN LXIX: TO THE LIQUID

1.
Thought, like an arrow, is set on the bow,
Like a calf, new born, at its mother's udder,
Wide-waved, the thought milks the tip of its course,
The liquid, toward its own vows, is released.

2.
The thought is shot, the wine is poured,
The force of the drink combusts in the mouth,
Clarity rings with a killer's roar,
A wine drop drips on the goatskin gourd.

3.
On the skin of the ewe, the mate-seeker, radiant,
The unfettered-one's daughter freed as he enters the way,
The dazzling gold resounds, joining divine drinker to drink,
Sharpening the male force, like a buffalo, he shines.

4.
The bull bellows, the cows, enflamed, answer his call,
To the gods, adorned and attending, the goddesses turn,
The liquid traverses the ewe's white skin,
Clothed, not with cloth, but with that which it cleansed.

5.
The dazzling gold, the immortal, emerging is clothed
In a cloth which does not age and which blinds,
He made, for the two cups, a carpet of clouds
And with great force, for emersion, the top of the sky.

6.
The rays, like sun's rays, eager to part,
Intoxicated, animated the soldiers of sleep,
And the fabric spread out—rapid emissions!
Without the burning no thing is clear.

7.
Rapid, as in a river's descending wave,
The liquors which rose from the bull found a way,
Joy in our hearts for the two and four-footed,
For us, O liquid, let the foods and harvest arise!

8.
Brighten the treasures, the streams of gold,
Horses, cows, wheat, and the dazzling force,
You—O you, liquid! You, my fathers, arise!
Chiefs of the sky, arise! Makers of nourishment!

9.
Illumined, these liquids, like chariots
In conquest, have gone to Indra, poured,
They pass through the ewe's radiant filter,
Rejecting the envelope the war horses of gold charge the rain.

10.
Brilliant drop! for the powerful Burning, alight!
Giver of joy! Destroyer! with absolute words!
Bring to your singer resplendent goods
That heaven and earth satiate us with gods!

KNOWLEDGE OF THE SELF*

*Extract from the Brihadaranyaka Upanishad,
IV 4, 10-21*

Into a blind darkness go
those dedicated to nonknowing;
into even deeper darkness go
those content with knowing.

"Without Joy" is the name of these worlds,
enveloped in blind darkness;
those without knowledge or reason
go, at the outset, to them.

If he knew himself,
if man could say: this is "I,"
by which desire, for which goal
would his body be enflamed?

He who has found himself, in whom the being
buried in the depth of this death has awakened,
he is all active, he is the author of all,
for him, the world—he is, himself, the world.

Here, as well, we must know this;
if not, ignorance, the great perdition.
Those knowing this become immortal,
the others, in misfortune, bury themselves.

---

*First published in *Bharata*, Paris, Éditions Gallimard, 1970.

RASA or Knowledge of the Self

When one has once recognized
this self, this god, suddenly,
this master of past and future,
one turns away no more.

That from which the year unwinds
in rounds of days,
the gods confess it light of lights
and immortal life.

That, foundation of five and five reigns,
that on which space reposes,
It is that I think of as the self,
I, who know the sacred word—I, without death, immortal.

Breath of breath and sight of sight,
hearing of hearing,
thought of thought—those who know it
have discerned the word, ancient, original.

It must be perceived by thought.
Nothing here exists separately.
He who sees things as separated
goes from death to death.

It must be perceived in its unity,
that, the immense, that, the stable,
beyond friction, traversing space,
the self, without birth, the great, the stable.

When the sage has recognized it,
let him attain its knowledge, Brahman.
Let him not be dispersed by numerous words:
for that is the weakening of the word.[1]

---

[1] To translate, here, is often to choose. "Self" for *atman*, "sacred word" for *Brahman*, "gods" for *devas*, mitigating a subtle play between the diverse values of these words. This translation aspires only to offer, to a reader who does not know Sanskrit, a directly accessible meaning.

SOME SANSKRIT TEXTS ON POETRY*

1.

The Utility of Poetry

(*Sahitya-darpana*, first section, entitled "The Essential Nature of Poetry," beginning:)

Aum! Salutations to Ganesha! At the beginning of this book, the author, to eliminate the obstacles to the complete success of his task, turns to the supreme authority in the matter of language—the divinity of language:

> 1. *Shining with beauty like the autumn moon,*
> *Removing the curtain of darkness in my spirit,*
> *May she, the goddess of words,*
> *Illumine the meaning of all things.*

The fruits of this book, which is in the service of poetry, will be the fruits themselves of poetry. We shall now cite these fruits.

> 2. *By virtue of poetry, the fruits of the quadruple*
> *(human) activity are easily grasped, even by those*
> *whose intelligence is limited; this is why we define*
> *the essential nature (of poetry) in this text.*

The "quadruple activity" refers to the "four kinds of motives" in human conduct: *dharma*—the search for the just and true; *kama*—the search for pleasure and emotional satisfaction; *artha*—the search for livelihood and material well-being; and finally *moksha*—the search for deliverance. One can also cite "three motives," excluding the fourth, which is of a superior order, "supramundane," the first three belonging to the natural order.

---

*First published in *Le Contre-Ciel*, Paris, Éditions Gallimard, 1943.

"Men of little intelligence," don't forget, are you and I, men gifted with a simple natural intelligence, who have not acquired by a special work the superior faculties of understanding.

"Grasped" must be understood in the sense of "gathered" or "comprehended," according to the doctrine of the author.

By virtue of poetry, the fruits of the quadruple activity are easily grasped, because it (poetry) compels us to behave like Rama and those like him and not like Ravana and those like him, and also because it (poetry) teaches us to do this and not that, to follow a certain example and to refuse another.

At first the author seems to interpret his words in a vulgar and apparently simple manner. But later we see that he is far from assigning a didactic role to poetry. With regard to the theater, he shows that this art—which is "audible poetry"—refines and edifies us by virtue of an "act of communion" which reunites the represented heroes, the actor, and the audience in a single moment of impersonal emotion, a moment of *rasa*. Poetry does not instruct as a professor does but through its power to transform the interior state.

...Poetry makes the just attainable, for example, when it induces us to praise the lotus feet of the Lord (Narayana, that is to say, Vishnu). "A single word, well-used and perfectly understood is, in heaven and the world, the cow to satisfy all desires"; such words, written in the knowedge (*Veda*) make the truth known: that poetry makes material goods attainable is also implied; and happiness as well through material goods and deliverance (it helps us to attain deliverance by compelling us *not* to consider the first three motives independently from the fourth).

Here again, a rather simple interpretation is presented: the poet exercises his profession for its material and emotional benefits. But the same poet, fully to realize his craft, must not forget the four goals, of which the last—deliverance from the chain of desire and action—dominates the first three by annihilating them. If he sought only one of these goals, the poet would be a teacher of morals, a public entertainer, a lover, or an ascetic. But one of the greatest poets of India, Bhartrihari, sings and lives within a single work and life, material pleasure, profane love, and ascetic devotion.

I admit that the way in which poetry speaks of the treasures of the heart (*kama*, which the author seems to understand as "pleasure" in general) is explained in a somewhat unsatisfactory way, but perhaps the author was anxious to proceed to other more important topics.

René Daumal

Due to an absence of "savor," the laws of the quadruple activity, as they are taught in the books of knowledge, are difficult to understand, even by those whose intelligence is fully matured. Poetry, by the milk of its supreme felicity, makes them easily understood, even by those whose intelligence is in a tender infancy. One might ask: of what virtue is poetry for those whose intelligence is matured, as the books of knowledge are accessible to them? This cannot be stated. If it is discovered that an illness, usually treated with bitter herbs, might also be treated with sugar candy, who, afflicted with this illness, would not choose the sugar candy treatment?

The excellence of poetry is expressed in the *Agni Purana*: "The state of man is difficult to attain in this world and knowledge is very difficult to attain; the state of the poet is difficult to attain, and creative power then is very difficult to attain."

It is stated in the *Vishnu Purana*: "The dramatic art is a means with which to realize the three forms of desire," and "all recited poetry and all chant, without exception, are aspects of Vishnu, of the great being, clothed in sonorous form."

(*Natya Sastra*, first reading, The Origin of the Theater:)
(At the beginning of the *kali-yuga*, the age of obscurity in which we live, the gods, distressed by the proliferation of the inferior castes to whom access to the sacred knowledge was forbidden and fearing the disorder that would result, went to Brahma and asked him to "produce a new *Veda*, accessible to men of all births." Brahma produced the dramatic art which contained all the arts. The saint Bharata, with his one hundred sons, was entrusted with the presentation of the first performance. It was performed to an assembly of *devas* and *asuras* who, by the vision of human disorder, had been finally reconciled. But Bharata's subject was somewhat unfortunate. He presented a performance of the great battle in which the *devas* defied the *asuras*. Offended, the *asuras* began, in the performance hall itself, to cast spells on the actors, and the battle was about to begin again for real. Brahma intervened and narrated the following discourse to the *devas* and *asuras*. Here he speaks to the *asuras*, sons of Diti:)

Enough of your resentment, Sons of Diti, relinquish your negativity.

The opposition of good and evil manifests in you and in the gods; it is the law which relates all states and actions.

The theater represents neither your nature nor that of the gods exclusively. It is a representation of the triple world in its entirety.

RASA or Knowledge of the Self

Sometimes law, sometimes play, sometimes profit, sometimes appeasement, sometimes laughter, sometimes war, sometimes desire, sometimes murder.

Law for those who follow the law, desire for those who are dedicated to desire, constraint for those who have no self-discipline, self-mastery for those who know how to behave.

To eunuchs it gives audacity, to braggarts energy; instruction to the ignorant, science to the learned.

Pastime of great lords, comfort for those struck by misfortune; wealth for those who live from wealth, courage for trembling spirits.

Containing all the diverse states, created from all the diverse situations, I created this theater as an analogy of the movement of the world.

(...)

There is no knowledge, no profession, no science, no art, no action—that will not be manifest in this theater.

Therefore, you have no right to be angry with the immortals. I have created this theater as an analogy of the seven continents.

The theater has been made in order to show, in their totality, the actions of devas and asuras, kings and men and visionary priests.

All individual natures in the world, with their particular forms of happiness and sorrow, with their gestures and means of expression—this will be called theater.

To sacred knowledge, to science and to myths, it will give an audience, and to the people, a diversion: such will be this theater.

René Daumal

2.

The Essence of Poetry

(*Sahitya-darpana*, first section, continuation:)

What, then, is the essential nature of poetry? To this question someone replied: "It is the union of sound and meaning, it is faultless, gifted with virtue, with and sometimes without ornaments."

This definition is from Mammata. The union of sound (or the vocable) and meaning is that which is called a word (*pada*). The "virtues" (*guna*) will be discussed further on; tentatively, we say that these are different tones which can manifest poetic expression. The author discusses point by point the proposed definition.

This requires reflection. If an absence of faults is necessary in order for poetry to exist, then it is necessary to refuse this quality to a stanza from Bhavabhuti which is tainted with a categorical fault, but which, because of its power of "resonance," belongs in fact to the highest order of poetry (adhering to the doctrine of the author in question).

The term "resonance" (*dhvani*) must be defined. Words have three "powers" of signification: literal meaning, derived figurative meaning, and suggested meaning. The first two suffice for ordinary speech and didactic discourse. But it is through a "suggestion," independent of the first two "powers," that the meaning of the poem is transmitted; and this "suggestion" is also called "resonance," or even "subordinate meaning."

One might reply that only a part of the poem is tainted with a fault (...), or that "without faults" means, in this context, "with very few faults." (These rather futile objections are easily refused: a composition, considered in its entirety, must be poetry or nonpoetry.) There are absolute faults, which always destroy the quality of poetry and nonabsolute faults—such as cacophony, etc. which, when they do not interfere with the "savor," the essence of the poem, are no longer faults (and which even can become ornaments) ... Finally, the presence or absence of faults cannot define poetry; and similarly, to define a pearl, one cannot allow the imperfections, such as the perforation of a worm, to influence the definition; these are accidents which do not remove the pearlness from the pearl (...).

It is equally inappropriate to introduce the "virtues" as specific qualities in the definition. For "virtues" are only functions of the savor (...) as heroism (and other "virtues") are functions of the spirit.

One notes, below, the definition of "savor"—conscious gustation of an objective emotion—which is the essence of poetry.

It is therefore necessary to define poetry by the "savor," and not by the "virtues," which are its properties. The presence of sounds and meanings which manifest the "virtues" in poetry are only conditions of its construction; they are not elements of its essential nature. It is said: "Of poetry, sound and meaning are the body, the savor is the spirit; the virtues are similar to heroism and other expressions of the spirit. The faults are like the impediment of blindness, the allures like different stances of the body, the ornaments like its bracelets and earrings."

"Allures" (*riti*, "the manner of flow") are types of stylistic mechanisms which constitute the interior rhythm of poetic expression. "Styles" if one wishes: but the poet must be capable of manipulating them all. The "ornaments" correspond approximately to our "rhetorical figures."

All definitions of this genre must be rejected for the same reason: they only enumerate the accessories which are, more or less, indispensable for poetry. And, regarding what is said by the author of the *Dhvani*, that "the essence of poetry is the resonance"—is it a question of the "resonance" (in the broad sense of the term), which is of three types, according to whether it suggests a material fact, an ornament or a savor, or only of that (resonance) which evokes the savor? In the first case, no! For it would then be necessary to include enigmas, etc. in the definition (....) In the second case, we say: amen! (....) Otherwise, the phrase "Theodore goes to the village" would be poetic because it suggests the servants and men who accompany (that person). If one maintains that "yes, it is poetry," then no! For the quality of poetry can be attributed only to that which has savor (...).

Also, in the *Agni Purana*, it is said: "However great the linguistic skill, only savor can animate (language)." (...) And the author of the *Dhvani* says: "It is not simply by recording that 'such and such happened' that a poet is a poet, because legends and stories do that very well." (...) If one tries to view as poetry compositions which are lacking savor, due to phenomena in them which manifest "virtues" or to the absence or faults or presence of ornaments, an inferior genre (only) of poetry will be the result (...).

René Daumal

And when Vamana says: "Allure is the essence of poetry," we say: no! As allure (*riti*) is one of the specific stylistic ordonnances, that is to say, (in the corporeal analogy previously described) comparable to physical posture, and totally devoid of "essence."

Finally, the author of *Dhvani* says: "A meaning acceptable to those who have a heart is that which constitutes the essence of poetry. Its two divisions are called: of literal meaning and of suggested meaning." This definition contradicts the author's own words, i.e., that the "resonance" (or suggestion) is the "essence of poetry"; it must therefore be rejected.

What, then, ultimately is poetry?

3. Poetry is a word whose essence is savor.

We will now explain the meaning of savor. Savor is "the essence" in terms of the substantial reality. That is to say, savor is the life itself of poetry; without it, there is *no* poetry. "Savor" (*rasa*) is, etymologically, that which is "savored" (*rasayate*). The term includes savor-emotions and savor-reflections as well (which are defined further on in the text).

4. The faults are that which veil it (poetry).

The faults, cacophony, superfluous words, etc. are analogous to infirmities, e.g., blindness or lameness, which affect (the person) through (the medium) of his own body: they affect (the poem) through sounds and meanings. Faults, such as calling the manifestation of an emotion by its technical name (instead of suggesting it through the power of resonance)—that is to say, "prosaicness," are like maladies, which directly affect (the person); they veil the savor which is the essence of poetry (…).

5. The virtues, ornaments, and allures are called "agents of construction."

(The corporeal analogy described above shows the way in which these agents "construct" the savor, and thus the poetry itself.)

3.

The Savor

(*Natya Sastra*, sixth reading, 32-33:)

Like gourmets, who when eating relish food mixed with condiments and diverse ingredients, the sages relish in spirit the principal emotions joined to their manifestations and their diverse means of expression. This is why these emotions (to the degree to which they are relished) are called the "savors" of the dramatic art.

"Savor" is therefore an emotion manifest through the means of art and consciously perceived. Considered as a moment of consciousness, the savor is one: it is indivisible. With relation to the emotions, which are its expressions, it manifests as many forms as there are principal emotions—eight or ten according to the author in question. They are distinguished as follows: erotic, comic, pathetic, furious, heroic, repugnant, and wondrous, in addition to, in certain authors, familial (paternal or maternal love) and tranquil (religious love).

According to the *Agni Purana*, savor is derived from the third form of the tri-unity in its metaphysical aspect, "being-consciousness-bliss," through the intermediary of the "self" and pleasure in general. Like the *Natya Sastra*, this same work admits four fundamental savors: erotic, furious, heroic, and repugnant, from which the other four are derived as antithetical or passive forms. But a dominant place is given to the erotic, which (asserting all the modulations of the pathos of love) became the principal savor in the works of Bhojaraja.

(*Rasatarangini*, VI—This text plagiarizes the *Dasarupa*, but I use it as the latter text is not available:)

A principal emotion, manifest in the representation of its determining aspects, exterior effects, bodily expressions, and accessory accompaniments, and savored in its full development is a savor. When (this representation) provokes an arrest (a repose) of the spirit—then it is a savor. Or again: the awakening in the consciousness of a fundamental emotion which is retained as a latent impression—this is a savor. That which provokes this reminiscence are the the determining aspects manifesting the emotion (the latent impression can otherwise, conforming to the general Hindu belief, have been received in "another existence").

There are two types of savor: mundane and nonmundane (natural and supernatural). The first is engendered through contact with elements of this world; the second is engendered through contact with nonmundane elements (…) and is regarded as knowledge (knowledge which has the character of reminiscence).

(The savor manifests in three domains: in dream, in imaginative play (or fantasy), and in art. Here we are concerned with the savor in art, but it is necessary to affirm the existence of the other two possibilities. For example, in the following stanza of Bhartrihari, the existence of a savor of imagination is affirmed:)

> *"Happy are those who inhabit mountain caves,*
>   *meditating on the supreme light,*
>
> *At these felicitous waters, birds without fear*
>   *in their huddled breasts, quench their thirst,*
>
> *But we who compose in the fantasy palace—ponds*
>   *and shores, parks, plays, and trifles,*
>
> *Curious distraction! We humor ourselves and thus*
>   *pass our lives in pure loss."*

(*Sahitya-darpana,* third section, 33 et seq.:)

A principal emotion, such as love, evoked through the representation of its determining aspects, exterior effects, and accompanying accessories, attains, for those who are conscious, the nature of savor.

> Now the savor will be described in essence; in its indivisible aspect of a moment of consciousness provoked by the occasion of an emotion.

Risen from the essential principle (*sattva,* the pure and luminous principle, the antithesis of *tamas,* the obscure and inert principle, and *rajas,* the intermediary and passionate principle), without division, shining in its own essence, created from (the union of) joy and knowledge, freed from contact with any other perception, twin sister and gustation of the divine, animated by the breath of supernatural admiration—this is savor, which some (having interior discrimination) relish as the proper, inseparable form of the self.

Savor is knowledge, "shining in itself" (…). It is joy, even in the representation of sorrowful events, even when it engenders tears (…) because it is a supernatural recreation of represented states (…). It is simple, like the taste of a complex dish. It can manifest as the reminiscence of a latent impression (*vasana*). It compels an act of "communion" between the actor (or poet), the represented heroes, and the audience. It does not exist beyond perception of it. It is not a production of a combination of preexisting elements. It has neither past, present, nor future. It is, thus, supernatural (not profane) (…) we know it only by savoring it.

("Supernatural admiration," amazement and expansion of the spirit, created by contact with a reality superior to this world, is the principle of all savor and is found in *all* true poetry.)

—1943

Appendix

THE FOUR CARDINAL TIMES

The black hen of the night
begins again to powder a dawn,
Salut, the white, salut the yellow
Salut, seed that one does not see.

Lord of Noon, King of an instant
strikes the gong at the height of day,
Salut, the eyes, salut, the teeth,
Salut, the devouring mask, forever.

On cushions of the horizon
the red fruit of memory,
Salut, sun who knows how to die,
Salut burner of impurities.

But in silence I salute the great midnight,
She who keeps watch while the three are in motion,
Closing the eyes I see her without seeing anything
   Beyond the darknesses
Closing the ear I hear her step that does not recede.

—René Daumal, 1944

About the Translator

Louise Landes Levi

Poet, musician, and translator, Louise Landes Levi (NYC) worked in the Daumal archives under the direct supervision of Claudio Rugafiori & H. J. Maxwell 1976-78 to produce *RASA*. In a recent interview with Brooklyn Rail (2019) she says "René Daumal was the first to realize that this text had a living message, a living energy for contemporary artists. The *rasas* are the aspects or varieties of aesthetic experience (…) the word is sometimes translated as 'flavors' or 'taste.'"

Louise's Mirabai translation *Sweet On My Lips: the love poems of Mirabai* (1997, repr. 2006), published by Cool Grove, was for her a direct application of the translation theories elucidated by Daumal in *RASA*.

Her other titles published by Cool Grove are *Guru Punk* (1999), *The Book L* (2010), & *Where I Stand in Angel* (2021).

Poetry and selected essays of René Daumal
translated by Louise Landes Levi

Memorables, Shambhala, 1974
& Longhouse, as a fold-out accordion, 2009

Yellow Laughter, Montana Gothic, 1977

The Four Cardinal Times, Montana Gothic, 1977

Program Notes for Orchestral Work, SUNY, 2013
& Ragged Lion, 2020

The Ass Between Two Chairs, Text, no. 7, 1978

On Indian Music and Concerning Uday Shankar,
Journal of the Sangeet Natak Akademi, 1978

RASA, New Directions, 1982 & Shivastan, 2003 & 2006

The Sacred War, Coronamundi, 2001

Poetry White, Poetry Black, Blank Forms Journal no. 7,
The Cowboy's Dreams of Home, 2021

AFTERWORD
A Form of Fire

The year is 1969 or 70. I hear
Sanskrit chant for the first

time, the guru of the ashram
in question houses me w. the
Indian ladies. I learn
Devanagari through non
didactic means,

I can read (but
not understand) Sanskrit . . .
I speak Hindi w. the women
& sing the Sanskrit chant,

I experience it as a
form of
FIRE

Roger Shattuck in his introduction to Mt. Analogue writes
similarly of Daumal's experience
w. Sanskrit letters.

I write to my cousin in Paris
for the Daumal texts—at the

time in BHARATA (Gallimard).
I'm of Romanian Armenian descent on
my mother's side, my cousins
are born in Paris, my
brother & I in
NYC

A few years later,
I'm in Delhi, boyfriend is
studying w. Dilip Chandra
Vedi, I make an effort to save our
relation by joining him for some months.

I realize that 2 sarangi players
in one partnership will not work, I sacrifice
my sarangi, with an erroneous understanding: A translator is
more lady like than a
sarangi player.
As a translator
he will still love me. He's fr.

family of famous musicians
in Amsterdam, my father was a cloth
salesman. His brothers are
violinists, he doesn't need
'competition.'

I translate 2 essays that
are later printed in Journal of

the Sangeet Natak Akademi,
'On Indian Music'
&
'Concerning Uday Shankar'

The relation fails but I continue
my translations of Daumal, 2 more essays
& some of the poems. This work is published
in various journals, the last unpublished piece,
this year by Blank Forms,
Poetry Black, Poetry White.

It's 1976.
Ira Cohen shows up in
Amsterdam. The 2 essays on
Indian Music are under my bed.
I have no idea what to do w. them
but I know someone will
come along who does,

That's Ira, my house
Guest. He takes me around
the city like his pet poet. Bill Levy,
another ex-pat says New Directions
will be interested
& they are.

Daumal had a close relation
to Alfred Jarry, he, RD, was born a few
months after Jarry's death. I show up at the Daumal

archives. Many academics have wanted
to translate the Sanskrit works but
are unable to get a contract.
I have a letter fr. New Directions
they are interested.

I was born a few months
after Daumal died. Not knowing
the Jarry/Daumal connection, I am sur-
prised & not really when the archivists
tell me I must have promised
Daumal, in the bardo to
translate this work.
ND renegs. They want
a famous academic to do it.
The archivists disagree & make it
impossible for anyone but LLL
to touch the material.

Various assistants come
to my rescue eg. Richard Leigh
& Heathcote Williams. After
6 years New Directions
publishes RASA

Thanks to Claudio
thanks to MAX Thanks

to Henri Michaux who was sure
the archivists wld. refuse
the newcomer, 'they

were serious'
&
who then supported
my translation in Paris.

All
subsequent work
drew its inspiration
fr. these texts.

LLL
Kyoto 2020

If

www.ingramcontent.com/pod-product-compliance
Lightning Source LLC
Chambersburg PA
CBHW030302100526
44590CB00012B/491